KAKADU

A WORLD HERITAGE OF UNSURPASSED BEAUTY

Australian National Parks and Wildlife Service

KAKADU
A world heritage of unsurpassed beauty

DERRICK OVINGTON

Australian Government Publishing Service
Canberra 1986

© Commonwealth of Australia 1986

ISBN 0 644 04064 5 Case-bound edition

Typeset by CPP Pty. Ltd. T/as Canberra Publishing and Printing Co., Fyshwick, A.C.T.
Printed by The Griffin Press Limited, Adelaide, S.A.

FOREWORD

Kakadu, an area of unique wilderness, contains almost 1000 species of plants, a great diversity of animals, more than a third of Australia's bird species, an abundance of Aboriginal sites and art works of haunting beauty: in short, it redefines our concept of a national park.

For me and my family, Kakadu has become a very special part of our lives. Over time each one of us, my wife Rae and my sons Stuart, Martin and Adam, have grown fond of this enchanting corner of Australia.

No series of photographs can fully do justice to the unsurpassed loveliness of such a park. However, Derrick Ovington's book goes a very long way towards capturing the essence of Kakadu. The text is informative, factual and written in the laconic style which accurately portrays Derrick's personality, and reflects his deep love for Kakadu.

The text and the photographs neatly complement one another, so the book is not just a collection of stunning images, but an account of Kakadu, its inhabitants, its history and its future.

It is essential that people be encouraged to visit Kakadu and to experience its wonders first hand. Management of the Park is vital for the maintenance of this treasure house with which nature has favoured us. The need for care in preserving the delicate ecological balance is made abundantly clear. It is for this reason, to preserve Kakadu for future generations, that it was inscribed on the World Heritage List by the UNESCO World Heritage Committee.

I know that the Park is in good hands. The rangers of the Australian National Parks and Wildlife Service are competent professionals who enjoy Kakadu; the quality of their work is indicative of their dedication.

I congratulate Derrick on having produced a first class book which will stimulate its readers to go and experience Kakadu for themselves.

BARRY COHEN
MINISTER FOR ARTS, HERITAGE AND ENVIRONMENT

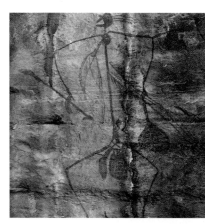

CONTENTS

Buffalo Hunters

Wildman River
Alligators NT
No photo Copyright

Historical photograph: Buffalo
hunters dining on a carcass.
(Australian Archives)

Historical photograph: A buffalo bull
making things hum.
(Australian Archives)

ACKNOWLEDGMENTS

This book would not have been possible
without the generosity of G. B. Baker
(G.B.B.), L. Barnett (L.B.), R. Garnett
(R.G.), D. A. Gillespie (D.A.G.), M.
Hallam (M.H.), I. P. Haskovec (I.P.H.),
R. W. G. Jenkins (R.W.G.J.), G. L. Miles
(G.L.M.), I. J. Morris (I.J.M.), M. Preece
(M.P.), C. Totterdell (C.T.) and P. Wellings
(P.W.) who permitted me to use their
excellent photographs of Kakadu National
Park and its inhabitants. The initials after
each photographic caption throughout the
text indicate the photographer. Ian Morris
and Colin Totterdell were particularly
helpful in giving me full access to their
extensive photographic collections.

Many members of the staff of the
Australian National Parks and Wildlife
Service shared their knowledge with me.
These include M. Alderson, N. Alderson,
M. F. Austin, G. B. Baker, L. Barnett, A. L.
Carter, V. Cooper, P. D. Coyne, J. Day,
M. A. Forbes, B. C. Gall, T. Gangali,
N. C. Gare, D. A. Gillespie, C. D. Haynes,
L. Hill, M. A. Hill, R. W. G. Jenkins, B.
Lawson, V. Lawson, G. L. Miles,
I. J. Morris, J. Namandali, B. Neiiji,
C. F. O'Brien, D. J. Phillips, G. D. Pike,
A. J. Skeat, H. Sullivan, P. Sullivan,
J. Wauchope and P. Wellings.
Dr R. W. Braithwaite of CSIRO kindly
provided me with unpublished data
collected as part of a consultancy with the
Australian National Parks and Wildlife
Service. S. M. Hazel, M. Rankin and N. M.
Regan patiently typed the text and the
figures were drawn by S. A. Craven.

Special thanks are due to the Honourable
Barry Cohen, M.P., the Minister for Arts,
Heritage and Environment, for his
encouragement and support.

J. W. Stokes kindly gave permission to
reproduce the historical photographs taken
in the early 1900's

Historical photograph: Buffalo hides
and horns. (Australian Archives)

Historical photograph: Wildman
River crocodiles. (Australian
Archives)

Historical photograph: Hauling in a
harpooned crocodile. Wildman River.
(Australian Archives)

A NATIONAL AND INTERNATIONAL HERITAGE

A heritage of beautiful plants. (M.P.)

Creation of Kakadu National Park   In 1979, Stage 1 of Kakadu National Park was proclaimed by His Excellency the Governor-General of the Commonwealth of Australia, Sir Zelman Cowen. This was the culmination of many years of effort by numerous people concerned to protect this unique area. The name, Kakadu, is derived from Gagadju, one of the several languages of the Aboriginal people whose traditional lands form part of the Park.

The considerable biological significance of the Alligator Rivers Region in the Northern Territory had been recognised previously when the Woolwonga Aboriginal Reserve was established in 1964 as a wildlife sanctuary of just over 500 square kilometres. However, the sanctuary did not satisfy conservationists and others who had long urged the creation of a major national park in the Region. This proved difficult to achieve and the situation became even more complicated in the early 1970s with the discovery of major uranium deposits, then some of the richest and most extensive in the world. Whilst uranium was seen as a potential boost for the mining industry and as a source of energy to overcome the so-called world energy crisis, the mining of uranium posed special environmental problems and had become a matter of public concern.

In order to resolve issues arising from the proposals to mine uranium, the Commonwealth Government set up the Ranger Uranium Environmental Inquiry. The Inquiry attracted considerable public interest and evidence was given by over 300 witnesses. The Commissioners conducting the Inquiry became involved in reconciling land use matters and minimising any potentially adverse social, cultural and biological consequences of mining and tourism. In their report to the Commonwealth Government in 1977 the Commissioners recommended that: uranium mining proceed at Ranger subject to strict environment

Escarpment seen from rainforest.
(C.T.)

1

controls; Aboriginal land rights be granted to part of the Alligator Rivers Region; and a major national park be established under Commonwealth legislation. These recommendations were accepted. Subsequently the traditional Aboriginal landowners leased much of their land for 100 years to the Director of the Australian National Parks and Wildlife Service to be managed as a national park for the benefit of the nation. Because of differences in legal standing, the Park had to be established in three stages (Fig. 1).

Stage 1 of Kakadu National Park, amounting to 6144 square kilometres, was proclaimed on 5 April 1979. Much of this is Aboriginal land but it includes areas to which Aboriginal land rights were not granted. Stage 2, an area of about 6929 square

Yellow faced cormorants. (I.J.M.)

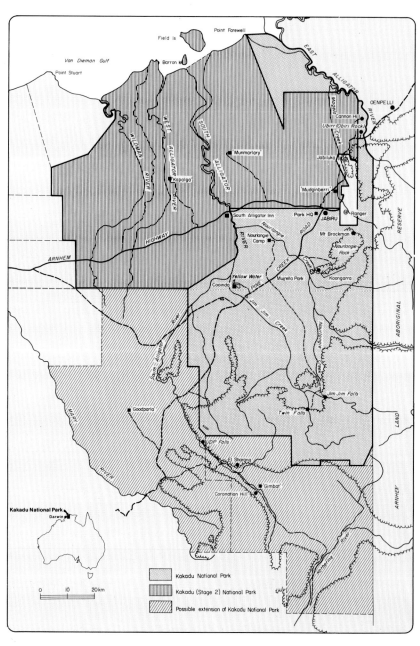

Fig. 1 Kakadu National Park

2

kilometres, was proclaimed on 28 February 1984. This consolidated the northern part of the Park and added wetland communities important as breeding grounds for many waterbirds. The proclamation of the southern Stage 3 of approximately 6000 square kilometres would add a new range of ecosystems to the Park, some of considerable tourist interest. With virtually all the water catchment of the South Alligator River included in the Park, the catchment can be managed as a unit to reduce soil erosion and water pollution. This provides greater protection to the vulnerable lowland wetlands of critical important to waterbirds and a variety of other wildlife.

The Park is not a continuous block because mining leases, particularly the uranium leases of Ranger, Jabiluka and

Mt Brockman, of great sacred significance with numerous rock art galleries. (I.J.M.)

Koongarra, are surrounded by, but not included in, it. Other leases excluded from the Park are those associated with the Border Store and the tourist facilities at Cooinda managed by the Aboriginal Gagadju Association. The new town of Jabiru, constructed primarily to accommodate uranium miners and their families, is within the Park but managed by an independent town authority with an elected council. The town land is leased from the Australian National Parks and Wildlife Service, which provided the basic design plan for the town.

Thus Kakadu National Park began, a product of personal conviction, extensive public discussion, Aboriginal generosity, parliamentary decision and finally proclamation by the Governor-General. Because of the comprehensive investigation

A heritage of Aboriginal rock paintings in various styles. Python cave. (I.J.M.)

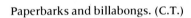

Paperbarks and billabongs. (C.T.)

4

Pelicans. (I.J.M.)

Sandstone massifs bedecked with rainforest. (C.T.)

leading to its establishment, many more Australians became aware of this treasure of unsurpassed beauty and of its international importance.

■

World Heritage Property   In 1980 the Australian Government nominated Stage 1, then the only area of the Park proclaimed, for inscription on the prestigious List of World Heritage Properties. The List is authorised under the UNESCO Convention concerning the Protection of the World Cultural and Natural Heritage. UNESCO requires independent confirmation that any proposed areas are of outstanding, universal value and worthy components of the world heritage. Detailed assessments are made by two international panels of experts, one to evaluate the cultural and the other the natural significance of all nominated areas. Remarkably, both panels separately supported the inclusion of Kakadu.

   After considering the panel reports, the UNESCO World Heritage Committee, at its October 1981 meeting, unanimously agreed that Stage 1 be inscribed on the List. The Committee also recommended the inclusion of additional stages of the National Park once they were proclaimed. Kakadu National Park has the distinction of being the first Australian area to be accepted as a World Heritage Property.

   Because of the wealth of birds they sustain, the wetlands of Kakadu are also on another United Nations List, that of Wetlands of International Importance especially as Waterfowl Habitat. This emphasises the great ornithological interest in the Kakadu

A refuge for magpie geese and other waterbirds. (C.T.)

A wetland of international importance. (C.T.)

A heritage of native animals. (I.J.M.)

wetlands and their key roles as bird breeding areas and as stop-over places for migratory birds.

■

Coming of people   The Kakadu panorama provides a revealing record of the powerful geological and biological evolutionary processes which, over the millenia, moulded the surface of the earth and generated a multitude of living things. Once people came and settled there, probably over 40 000 years ago, the pristine wilderness of Kakadu, rich in genetic resources, underwent further change. Kakadu has much to contribute to our knowledge of the evolutionary processes and the history and impact of the first human colonisation of the island continent.

    Some wildlife species became extinct during the period of Aboriginal occupancy, possibly because of hunting or habitat

Twin Falls Creek above the escarpment. (C.T.)

Twin Falls. (C.T.)

Broken escarpment. (C.T.)

Pelicans in flight. (I.J.M.)

Little black cormorants at
billabong. (I.J.M.)

change induced by people. The demise of these species could
also be due to the major climatic shifts and the resultant
environmental changes which occurred during that time. The
consequences of long-term climatic changes on the vegetation
and the associated animals were considerable. For example, less
than 1500 years ago, the area around Yellow Water Billabong
was a system of saline mud flats. Now, with a warmer climate,
this has been replaced by freshwater swamps and billabongs.

Increasingly, it is being recognised that Aborigines actively
managed the land. The environmental changes brought about by
Aboriginal people were less dramatic than those caused by other
indigenous people elsewhere because of Aboriginal land
management practices. Australian Aborigines have a remarkably
close affinity with the land and the natural resources it supports.
Of necessity, the traditional Aboriginal way of living is based on
sustainable use of the naturally occurring plants and animals of
vital importance to them as food and to make clothing,
adornments, weapons, fish traps and other objects. The major
impact of Aborigines on the environment resulted from the use
of fire in burning off the vegetation.

Progressively over thousands of years, a lifestyle evolved in
which Aboriginal people rarely stayed in the same place for more
than a few weeks but went to different locations where plant
material was available for gathering and animals for hunting.
The annual pattern of movement of Aboriginal people within
their clan territories and the kinds of plants and animals they

8

utilised were largely determined by the yearly rhythm of sequential climatic and biological change. Because of this local migration and cultural restraints, no area was exploited beyond its natural capacity for renewal.

Europeans only recognise two annual climatic periods, the wet and dry seasons. Possessing a lifestyle finely tuned to environmental conditions and a long experience of living off the land, Aboriginal people came to discern six major periods affecting their daily lives throughout the year (Fig. 2). The more refined Aboriginal perception of the climatic regime is enabling park management to be more finely adjusted to the various moods of Kakadu. For example, the implementation of certain park management operations, such as controlled burning, is

Paperbark and pandanus trees mirrored in still waters. (C.T.)

9

Ancient ripple marks on sandstone reveal its aquatic origin. (C.T.)

A natural rock bridge frames a panorama of plains and plateau. (C.T.)

being based increasingly on recognition of the relevance of the Aboriginal calendar in identifying the best times to burn.

People now come to Kakadu from many directions and in increasing numbers. Aboriginal people mainly enter the Park from the east, where the boundary of Kakadu adjoins the Arnhem Land Aboriginal Reserve. Non-Aboriginal visitors come mostly from the west through Darwin, about 250 kilometres distant, via the Arnhem Highway, an all-weather road. With the upgrading of the Pine Creek Road more people are entering the Park from the south. Others fly into Jabiru airport from Darwin.

■

Climate   As for other areas having a tropical monsoon climate, there are pronounced dry and wet seasons. The dry season is from May to September and the wet season from November to March, with April and October being transitional months. High temperatures prevail throughout the year, the average daily temperature generally being within the range 20 to 35°C and rarely less than 17°C. In October, temperature and humidity increase and the black thunderclouds and spectacular lightning displays foreshadow the wet to come. November brings violent thunderstorms and torrential rains begin in December or January. When it rains it pours. On average, about 1350 millimetres of rain falls each year, usually as heavy, long-lasting cloudbursts from January to March. In general, precipitation decreases southwards. An examination of cyclone tracks has revealed that at least six cyclones crossed over the area and eleven passed nearby in the sixty-year period ending June 1975.

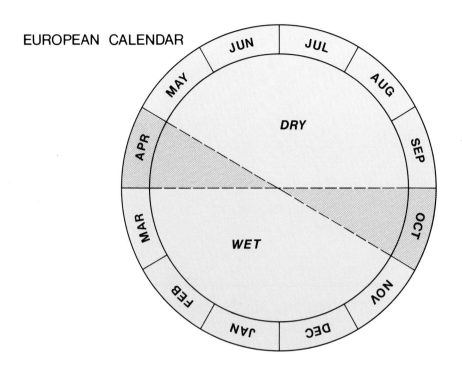

EUROPEAN CALENDAR

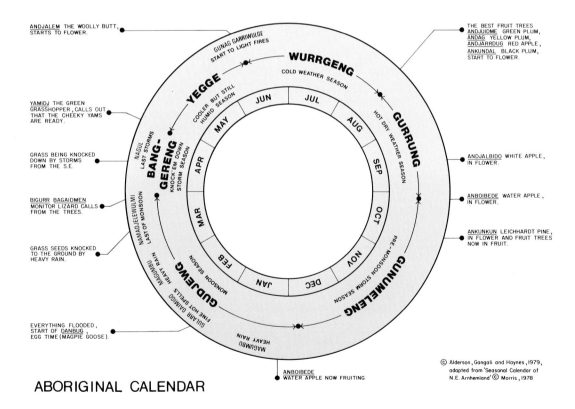

ANDJALEM THE WOOLLY BUTT, STARTS TO FLOWER.

THE BEST FRUIT TREES ANDJUIDME GREEN PLUM, ANDAG YELLOW PLUM, ANDJARRDUG RED APPLE, ANKUNDAL BLACK PLUM, START TO FLOWER.

GUNAG GARRIWULGE START TO LIGHT FIRES

WURRGENG
COLD WEATHER SEASON

YEGGE

COOLER BUT STILL HUMID SEASON

YAMIDJ THE GREEN GRASSHOPPER, CALLS OUT THAT THE CHEEKY YAMS ARE READY.

BANG-GERENG
KNOCK 'EM DOWN STORM SEASON

GURRUNG
HOT DRY WEATHER SEASON

GRASS BEING KNOCKED DOWN BY STORMS FROM THE S.E.

NAGUL LAST STORMS

ANDJALBIDO WHITE APPLE, IN FLOWER.

BIGURR BAGAIDMEN MONITOR LIZARD CALLS FROM THE TREES.

NAMADJELEWULMI LAST OF MONSOON

ANBOIBEDE WATER APPLE, IN FLOWER.

GRASS SEEDS KNOCKED TO THE GROUND BY HEAVY RAIN.

ANKUNKUN LEICHHARDT PINE, IN FLOWER AND FRUIT TREES NOW IN FRUIT.

GUDJEWG

MAGUMBU HEAVY RAIN

MONSOON SEASON

GUNUMELENG
PRE-MONSOON STORM SEASON

GULARR GAMIDJ FINE HOT SPELLS

EVERYTHING FLOODED, START OF DANBUG, EGG TIME (MAGPIE GOOSE).

MAGUMBU HEAVY RAIN

ANBOIBEDE WATER APPLE NOW FRUITING

© Alderson, Gangali and Haynes, 1979, adapted from 'Seasonal Calendar of N.E. Arnhemland' © Morris, 1978

ABORIGINAL CALENDAR

Fig. 2 European and Aboriginal calendars

11

Rainforest. (C.T.)

In October black thunderclouds
foreshadow the rains to come. (I.J.M)

Kakadu in the wet is a green, steaming environment and people from temperate areas may find climatic conditions particularly difficult and tiring. It is important to dress appropriately and not to become overstressed by too much physical activity. From a climatic point of view, the most pleasant time to visit the Park is from May to August when cooler conditions prevail and, with the ending of the rains, the floods have receded, making it easier to move around by road.

■

A very special place Timeless Kakadu is fascinating and spectacularly photogenic. Clearly it is a very special place, a beautiful and unusual wilderness with superb scenery. Nationally, it is seen by many as the most important national park of tropical, if not all, Australia. Internationally, it is accepted as a key component of the global heritage, with world recognition fully justified on the basis of either its cultural or natural attributes. Such widespread acclaim places a great responsibility on Australians to manage the Park wisely and to husband its resources.

Wise management requires a sensitive insight and appreciation of the varied faces and moods of Kakadu. Here, it is only possible to provide a glimpse of the grandeur and heritage that is Kakadu and a brief introduction to the management regime established to protect this natural wonderland for present and future generations of people to appreciate and enjoy. Australian possession and use of unique and inherently beautiful Kakadu must not jeopardise its future, for privileged custodianship carries with it accountability.

Spectacular lightning displays
illuminate the October scene. (I.J.M)

A HERITAGE OF LANDSCAPES

Canvas of landscapes   Kakadu National Park is large; it extends almost 200 kilometres from north to south and over 100 from west to east. Four major rivers, namely the Wildman and the West, South and East Alligator Rivers, cross the Park. Fed by a vast network of creeks, in the wet season they carry a huge volume of water from the Arnhem Land Plateau to Van Dieman Gulf.

Within the Park boundaries there is a remarkable canvas of landscapes, exciting and visually stimulating. The endless variety of Park scenery spans an immense geological time for the sandstone rocks of the plateau are almost 2000 million years old. In contrast, the coastal and riverine sediments are still accumulating as water-borne material is deposited after being carried by the rivers from the hinterland. Very rarely does a national park give such a feeling of untouched wilderness and have such a range of very different landscapes as does Kakadu.

There are six major landscape types, namely coastal swamps, tidal flats, floodplains, lowland hills, escarpment and plateau. All have many variants depending on a multiplicity of combinations of aspect, elevation, geology, soil, water and human influence. Whilst each landscape variant has its own individual character, all the landscapes are interrelated in one way or another. A good illustration of the ecological importance of this relationship is provided by animals which range widely and whose existence depends on using the resources of several landscape types at different times.

Coastal swamps   The northern coastal landscape is generally flat, with extensive mud banks offshore. Occasionally low sand dune ridges, covered with semi-deciduous monsoon forest, occur along the coast. The most striking feature of the coastal landscape is the fringing, dark green strip of evergreen mangrove swamps, which also lines the tidal river margins. Being subject to tidal flooding the mangrove swamps have wet, saline, mud soils. Access is difficult due to the apparently bottomless mud

Tranquil scene of rock, water and vegetation. (C.T.)

Jim Jim Falls. (G.L.M.)

15

and the tangle of tree stems and roots. Because of the dense tree canopy, the interior is generally gloomy and humid.

Not surprisingly, mangrove swamps are generally regarded as unpleasant places. Most people see them as havens for dangerous animals such as crocodiles, venomous snakes and poisonous insects. However, the mangroves are an important landscape component, providing a protective barrier which reduces coastal erosion and minimises the damaging effects of storm surges and the landward influx of saline water. Perhaps even more important, mangrove swamps are breeding places and refuges for much marine and bird life. Without them, the stocks of many species of fish and crustaceans, some highly prized, would be depleted.

A coastal landscape of mangroves and forested dunes backed by tidal flats. (C.T.)

Billabong. (I.J.M.)

Tidal flats   Inland from the coast there are extensive tidal flats formed of sea and river deposited alluvial mud. In the dry season, the slow-flowing rivers meander in great loops across the mud between raised natural levees of coarser sand. The more saline areas, being without a vegetation cover, are exposed as monotonous, level expanses of dark, mud soil. Baked incessantly by the tropical sun, the surface soil hardens and cracks in the aridity of the dry season. At high tides in the wet season, the river levees in some areas are overtopped and sometimes breached, causing widespread flooding with salt water.

Few plants can withstand the tidal flat combination of high salinity and extremes of dryness and flooding. A distinct vegetation zonation is associated with the decrease in salinity and flooding away from the coast and estuaries. A low vegetation characterised by samphire *Arthrocnemum leiostachyum* occurs in the innermost inland zone of the tidal flats.

Floodplains   Landwards, the tidal flat landscape in turn merges into one of broad, freshwater floodplains with a complex system of billabongs, creeks and rivers. The higher land to the east and south constitutes an enormous catchment from which water quickly discharges on to the floodplains once the rains begin. Then the lazy, meandering rivers and creeks overflow their banks causing a violent transformation of the floodplain scene, with much of the area submerged under a flood of moving fresh water. The higher hills and rock outcrops become islands

The East Alligator River meanders across the floodplains. (C.T.)

Floodplain. (I.J.M.)

Vast mudbanks border the shoreline and rivers. (C.T.)

17

Giant termite mounds scattered across grassland plain. (C.T.)

Land-locked billabongs in lowland hill landscape. (C.T.)

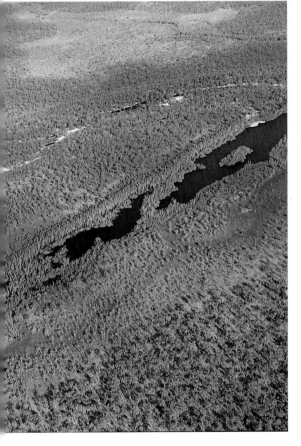

South Alligator River floodplains in the wet season. (C.T.)

isolated by vast tracts of water and provide refuge for many animals as they escape the rising water. Later, with the ending of the rains, the water level drops, the billabongs, rivers and creeks reappear and the draining and drying out of the soaked countryside commences.

Blanketed by a largely unbroken vegetation mantle, the flat floodplains are very productive biological systems and throb with life in the wet. Many kinds of plants and animals are present and the populations of some are very abundant. Sedges, herbs and paperbark trees dominate.

Floodplain landscape of billabongs and paperbark swamps. (C.T.)

Rock outliers left behind as the plateau eroded. Ubirr (Obiri Rock). (C.T.)

Lowland hills   To the west and south of the floodplains is a lowland hill landscape largely free of flooding. Undulating plains are interspersed between rocky hills and ridges and the vegetation is a mosaic of grassland, savannah and open eucalypt woodland reflecting local differences in environmental conditions. Past overstocking by cattle and failure to control buffalo numbers have left a legacy of soil erosion. At wetter, sheltered places, where fire rarely if ever penetrates, pockets of dense monsoon rainforest persist, their dark green colour contrasting with the glaucous greens and browns of the surrounding dry sclerophyll eucalypt woodland.

The escarpment is a major landscape feature. (C.T.)

Escarpment   To the east the lowland hills are overshadowed by the most dominant of all the landscape features, the precipitous sandstone escarpment of the Arnhem Land Plateau, which traverses the Park from north to south. Weathering has caused the escarpment to be greatly convoluted and to vary in form from sheer cliffs to stepped rock promontories with long talus slopes of broken rock below. Majestic and mysterious, with a myriad of aspects, colours and textures, the fluted escarpment face winds circuitously for over 500 kilometres through the Park. Illuminated by the sun's rays the exposed rock faces are warm red or bright cream in colour and with the setting of the sun gradually become golden brown. A few trees and shrubs cling precariously to the escarpment, their roots penetrating deeply into cracks in the sandstone rock for support and water.

In the wet season several streams cascade over the escarpment as spectacular waterfalls, adding an imposing landscape

dimension of great beauty. Although most waterfalls vanish in the dry season, some persist throughout much of the year. One of the best known of these, Jim Jim Falls, drops a sheer 200 metres into a seemingly bottomless, boulder-strewn pool.

Sandstone blocks perched one upon another. (C.T.)

Plateau Beyond the escarpment is the rocky landscape of the Arnhem Land Plateau, apparently stretching endlessly eastwards far beyond the Park boundary. More than 500 metres above sea level at its highest point, the plateau rises about 300 metres over the neighbouring lowland hill country. The plateau is composed mainly of middle Proterozoic quartz sandstone superimposed over even older volcanic, metamorphic and granitic rocks. The sandstone was deposited in a shallow sea almost 2000 million years ago and subsequently was consolidated by tectonic pressure. Ripple marks on some exposed surfaces provide evidence of its aquatic origin.

Deep gorges give access to the plateau. (C.T.)

The Arnhem Land Plateau, rugged and awe inspiring. (C.T.)

The crossbedded, multijointed, sedimentary sandstone rock layers progressively break up into huge, angular blocks. Rock pinnacles abound and display an infinite variety of shapes, with immense rock slabs perched one upon another sometimes appearing to defy the laws of gravity. Deep, steep sided valleys cut by ancient rivers and creeks along rock joints and faultlines penetrate far into the plateau broadly at right angles to the escarpment edge. The plateau is crisscrossed by an intricate, rectangular network of crevices etched out along the sandstone rock joints and variable in size. Being moister and cooler than the exposed rock and having some soil, the valleys and crevices invariably support vegetation, their verdant green accentuating the stark barrenness of the plateau rock environment.

Under the impact of ceaseless weathering and rock spalling, the plateau is receding south-eastwards leaving in its wake isolated, massive outliers of more resistant rock. Typical of such outliers are Mount Brockman and the smaller Ubirr (Obiri Rock). The plateau is believed to be retreating generally at up to 1 metre per 1000 years. In places, the undermining of cliffs by erosion causes massive collapsing of the plateau edge and a limited, temporary quickening of the retreat followed by a prolonged period of cliff stability.

Wilderness   The Kakadu landscapes give an impression of unchanging permanency but this is misleading because over the ages they have undergone enormous transformations as a result of weathering and major climatic shifts which affected the hydrology of the area. Furthermore, the Kakadu scenery is not completely natural in that it bears some imprint of human impact. Once people appeared on the scene, they began to bring about change.

Nevertheless, a common feature of all Kakadu landscapes is that they impart a feeling of natural wilderness and solitude. Kakadu is one of the few remaining areas where it is possible to escape from the stresses of modern living and to savour the joys of relaxing in essentially natural surroundings and experiencing the varied moods of nature. The landscapes of Kakadu are priceless wilderness assets whose value will be enhanced as other remote areas throughout the world are transformed by modern technology because of population pressure. As such they are an irreplaceable legacy to be protected for this and future generations of people to behold.

23

A HERITAGE OF CULTURE

Aboriginal settlement   Kakadu is an early, and possibly one of the earliest, human settlement areas of the Australian continent. Undoubtedly, Aboriginal people have lived at Kakadu for tens of thousands of years. Traditionally, Aboriginal people believe their occupation dates back to the dreamtime when landscapes and living things were created. According to the ancient lore, the acts of creation, by which the land was given form and life, were carried out by many creative beings. The stories of how this happened are well known by local Aborigines.

The first being of the creative era is Warramurrungundji, a female who came from the sea to the north-east and formed the landscapes. During her travels, she left spirit children in various places and instructed them on the language they were to speak. She also distributed various plant foods such as yams, spike rushes, red lilies and wild rice. At the end of her travels, Warramurrungundji turned into a rock, which is her djang or dreaming. Gurri, the blue tongued lizard, another of these creative beings, is said to have created the djang, totemic sites, of all the animal and plant species.

Djang places occur all over the Park and are permanent reminders to Aboriginal people of the reality and activities of the creation heroes. Some djang places can be open to the public but others are considered dangerous by Aboriginal people and to be avoided.

Most of our knowledge of the ancient Aboriginal culture of the Park comes from three main sources: accounts given by Aboriginal people and the early European explorers; archaeological digs at old occupation sites; and the interpretation of paintings at Aboriginal rock art sites.

It is evident from the accounts of Aborigines and explorers that the Aborigines of Kakadu customarily travelled around their territories for various purposes. These travels were not haphazard but in general were finely tuned to the changing seasons and the harvesting of the products of the land and water.

Post-estuarine contact period. European with hands on hips. Ubirr (Obiri Rock). (C.T.)

Mabuyu, a spirit carrying a collecting bag, goose wing fan, spears and spear thrower. Ubirr (Obiri Rock). (C.T.)

25

Pre-estuarine period, naturalistic style. Large painting of freshwater crocodile. Mt Brockman. (I.P.H.)

Pre-estuarine period, naturalistic style. Ancient thylacine painting damaged by waterflow. Ubirr (Obiri Rock). (C.T.)

At certain times of the year the Aborigines sought the welcome shelter of the multitude of cool caves and rock overhangs along the escarpment edge and around the marginal rock outliers. During these interludes, but also at other times, Aboriginal artists painted on the smooth rock surface. At regular camping sites stone tools and other objects, such as animal bones left from meals, became buried in the soil and this provides an important chronological record of Aboriginal occupation and lifestyles.

With such an abundance of art sites it is surprising that there are relatively few Aboriginal rock engravings at Kakadu. The several extensive stone arrangements present may have served as meeting places for the different clans or places where important rituals were held.

Stone arrangement of unknown age, possibly pre-estuarine. Cannon Hill. (I.P.H.)

Pre-estuarine period, dynamic style. An emu cries out after being speared by a hunter hiding behind grass or sticks. Mt Brockman. (I.P.H.)

Pre-estuarine period, dynamic style. Female figure with dilly bag and spear. Deaf Adder. (I.P.H.).

Archaeological excavations While addressing the Commissioners of the Ranger Uranium Environmental Inquiry, the late Mr Silas Roberts, then the Chairman of the Aboriginal Northern Land Council, stated: 'It is true that people who are belonging to a particular area are really part of that area and if that area is destroyed they are destroyed.' The links between Aboriginal people and the land have proved to be remarkably enduring despite the strains imposed particularly over the last century. Aboriginal people feel a strong responsibility to ensure the land is disturbed as little as possible, both for the physical health of the environment and for the spiritual and religious good of the landscape.

Understandably, the excavation of prehistoric deposits by archaeologists is a matter of some sensitivity. The traditional Aboriginal landowners are apprehensive of the disruption caused to sites occupied by their ancestors and left undisturbed for such a long time. Usually they want Aborigines to be present at excavations to look after their interests. In the longer term, Aborigines may wish to gain archaeological expertise so as to better contribute to and oversee any archaeological investigations. Researchers have come to recognise these concerns and the need to plan and co-ordinate archaeological studies to obtain as much information as possible without inadvertently wasting the irreplaceable archaeological material of the occupation sites.

Archaeological research began in earnest at Kakadu in the 1960s. Using the scientific technique known as carbon dating, some camping places have been shown to have been used by Aborigines for at least 23 000 years. This spans a thousand human generations and is clear evidence of the length and permanency of human occupation of tropical Australia.

Artefacts of great archaeological interest have been discovered. Excavations at old Aboriginal living sites have revealed that edge-ground stone axes were being made at Kakadu around 20 000 years ago. This is one of the earlier records of stone grinding technology in the world. Compared with their contemporaries elsewhere in the world, it appears that the Kakadu Aborigines were then technically well advanced. Implements of greater sophistication, such as unifacially and bifacially flaked stone points, found in the upper soil layers, were made some 4500 years ago. More recent tools of bone and shell have been found in the uppermost soil at some occupation sites.

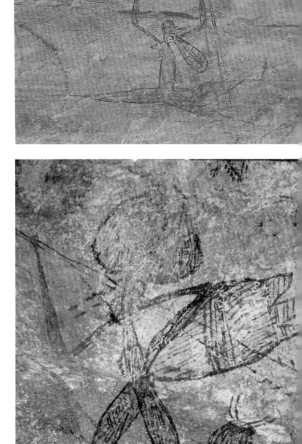

Pre-estuarine period, dynamic style. Male figure with elaborate head-dress, flowing skirt and spears. Burrunguy (Nourlangie Rock). (P.W.)

27

Pre-estuarine period, simple figures style. Small drawings of people in stick-like form with head-dresses below arm of larger male figure. Djaymuju. (I.J.M.)

Estuarine period, early X-ray style. Dolphin. Burrunguy (Nourlangie Rock). (C.T.)

Estuarine period. Jabiru storks with fish. Cannon Hill. (I.J.M.)

The interpretation of archaeological findings needs to be linked with evidence of environmental change. The environment in which the first people lived over 20 000 years ago was very different from that of today. With much of the world's water locked up in the polar ice caps, the sea level was considerably lower and the seashore 300 kilometres further north. The Kakadu area was then part of a vast inland plain, probably much drier than today and perhaps covered in low woodland. Some 8000–10 000 years ago, things began to change. As the global temperature increased, the ice caps melted and the sea level rose slowly, reaching its present level about 6000 years ago. As this happened the river valleys were flooded and salty estuarine conditions prevailed some distance inland. At the same time rainfall increased, enabling the development of forest and other plant communities similar to those now present in the Park.

These major environment changes meant that new resources became available to the Aboriginal people of Kakadu. This is shown at old camp sites, which, with rising sea levels, became near the sea or tidal rivers. Layers of shells or 'middens' then accumulated from the remains of meals. Examination of these 'middens' shows Aboriginal people hunted a wide range of animals including wallabies, bandicoots, possums, birds, salt and freshwater fish, crabs and a variety of reptiles. The remains of plant foods such as species of water lily, spike rushes and fan palms have been found at old camp sites of this period.

Archaeological investigations have revealed that a major change in the Aboriginal tool kit occurred about 4000–5000 years ago. This was the introduction of small stone points, thought to have been used as spear tips. Points made from mammal bones were also used, probably as spear tips for multiple-pronged fishing spears. Shells were used as cutting and scraping tools. Remnants of wooden implements have also been found in sites of this period.

About 1500 years ago freshwater environments began to replace the salty estuarine conditions on the floodplains. This resulted in an increased population of waterbirds such as magpie geese and whistling ducks. These birds and their eggs became a major component of the diet of Aboriginal people. The presence of large Aboriginal camp sites on the floodplain margins reflects the intensive use of the plant and animal resources of these freshwater wetlands.

This long history of Aboriginal occupation has resulted in the rich array of Aboriginal sites present in the Park today. They include spectacular rock art sites such as Ubirr (Obiri Rock) and key archaeological sites such as the Anbangbang site at Burrunguy (Nourlangie Rock). Undoubtedly, further research will improve our knowledge of the prehistoric settlers of Kakadu. Interest centres especially on learning more of how they coped with the great environmental changes following major climatic shifts and the relocation of the shoreline across the flat coastal plain. Already some information about this has been provided by studies of the chronology of rock paintings in the Park.

Post-estuarine period. Mythological figure, Mandjawilpil, an Owl Man. Deaf Adder. (C.T.)

Aboriginal rock art　One reason for the World Heritage status of Kakadu is the profusion of Aboriginal rock art sites, now recognised as a major international cultural resource. The sandstone rock provided a suitable surface on which to paint important events and features. The ceilings, walls and rocks of many caves and overhangs at Kakadu are adorned with vivid Aboriginal paintings, often painted one over the other. At some sites, there are extensive galleries of art in good condition. Elsewhere only traces of individual paintings remain. These paintings, at some 5000 art sites in the Park, are probably the oldest and greatest collection of early human artistic creativity. As such, they are unrivalled in the world. They are both a manifestation of an ancient Aboriginal culture and a tangible part of the life of living people.

Aboriginal painters used three main colours for their rock paintings: white, yellow and red. White pigment was obtained from pipe clay, kaolinite and allied minerals, all common through the area. The yellow pigment is probably limonite (hydrated iron oxide) and the red pigment haematite (anhydrous iron oxide). Both pigments are available in natural rocks or in pebbles. Black pigment, obtained from charcoal, was only rarely used in rock painting. The natural pigments were prepared by grinding the raw material to a fine powder on rock surfaces. After mixing with water, the pigment was applied to rock surfaces with brushes made of human hair, plant stalks or feathers. Alternatively the pigment was smeared on the rock surface with the hand, or blown from the mouth. Sometimes the

Post-estuarine period. Namarrgan the Lightning Man encircled by lightning produced by striking rocks with the axes protruding from the head and joints. Burrunguy (Nourlangie Rock). (C.T.)

rock face was struck with plants covered with pigment. In recent paintings at Burrunguy (Nourlangie Rock), a remarkable innovative approach was adopted in which European wash-house blue was used to colour the paintings.

The first European discovery of the rock art was by the expedition led by the explorer Ludwig Leichhardt in 1845 on his epic journey from Moreton Bay in Queensland to the ill-fated Victoria settlement of the Cobourg Peninsula. Since then, many more Aboriginal art sites have been found. The Australian National Parks and Wildlife Service has arranged for the paintings to be photographed using a special technique which gives three-dimensional photographs. This is providing a permanent, detailed reference record for future study.

30

Fig. 3 Chronology of Aboriginal rock art

YEARS AGO	PERIOD	PHASE	KEY STYLE
— 35 000 —	PRE-ESTUARINE		Prints of hands, grass and other objects pressed or thrown against rock surfaces.
— 30 000 —			
— 25 000 —			
— 20 000 —		NATURALISTIC	Large naturalistic animals and humans.
			Dynamic figures
		STYLISATION	Post dynamic figures
— 15 000 —		SCHEMATISATION	Simple figures
		SYMBOLISM	Yam figures
— 10 000 —			
	ESTUARINE	REALISM	X Ray descriptive
— 5 000 —			
	POST-ESTUARINE • FRESHWATER		X Ray decorative
— 1 000 — — 0 —	• CONTACT	CASUAL	

Post-estuarine period. Namandi, a malignant spirit. Burrunguy (Nourlangie Rock). (C.T.)

Evidently, both the rock art styles and motifs changed through the thousands of years of Aboriginal occupation and our present knowledge of the paintings owes much to the devoted, painstaking work of George Chaloupka, who has catalogued and interpreted them. He clarified the chronology of different art styles and elucidated their cultural setting in terms of the changing social and physical environments of the Aboriginal people. Chaloupka identified four main art periods in the following chronological sequence: the oldest is the pre-estuarine, followed by the estuarine and the post-estuarine, subdivided into the freshwater and contact periods.

Post-estuarine period. Spirit figures. Burrunguy (Nourlangie Rock). (C.T.)

31

Post-estuarine period. Hand stencils produced by blowing a pigment solution from the mouth over hands pressed on rock. Nangalwur. (C.T.)

Post-estuarine period. Dynamic frieze of hunters carrying spears and goose wing fans. Ubirr (Obiri Rock). (C.T.)

Pre-estuarine period The pre-estuarine period ended around 8000 years ago and predates the last glaciation (Ice Age), which was at its maximum about 18 000 years ago. The climate was drier and the sea level about 150 metres lower than now. Consequently, the Arnhem Land Plateau was over 300 kilometres from the coast and the vegetation of the extensive flat plain, exposed by the drop in sea level, would be savannah-like with grassland and scattered clumps of trees. Six distinct art styles typical of this period have been recognised and represent a remarkable evolution from natural to more stylised paintings.

The most ancient paintings were made by coating hands, grass seeds and other objects with wet pigment and pressing or sticking them against the rock surface to form positive prints. Sometimes positive prints were obtained by throwing objects coated with wet pigment against a rock face.

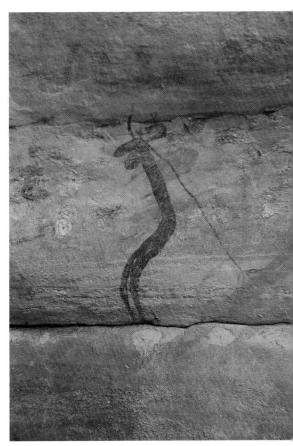

Post-estuarine period. Female spirit figures over older paintings. Burrunguy (Nourlangie Rock). (C.T.)

Post-estuarine period. Graceful female figure. Mt Brockman. (I.P.H.)

The next style is characterised by large naturalistic paintings of people and animals first drawn in detailed outline and then filled in with an ochre wash. People are also depicted as one-line-thick, sticklike figures hunting animals with simple or three-pronged multibarbed spears. Many kinds of animals portrayed then can still be found at Kakadu — wallabies, possums, bandicoots, echidnas, pythons and freshwater crocodiles.

Remarkably, some paintings are thought to represent animals of the Australian megafauna known to have become extinct around 30 000 years ago. Other animals drawn, such as thylacines and long beaked echidnas, survive elsewhere but are known to have been absent from the Australian mainland and Kakadu for thousands of years, thus further emphasising the great age of these paintings. Biologists believe thylacines once occurred throughout Australia, but became restricted to the island of Tasmania with the introduction of dingoes to mainland Australia by Aborigines perhaps 5000 years ago. Dingoes replaced thylacines as the main predators of the mainland fauna but failed to reach Tasmania because of the Bass Strait sea barrier. Similarly long beaked echidnas have been absent from Australia for thousands of years. A remnant population of this once widespread species still survives in the Highlands of New Guinea.

The next style of the pre-estuarine period is represented by dynamic figures of humans, animals and animal-headed beings. These relatively small drawings are remarkably expressive and skilfully depict motion associated with normal everyday activities such as a hunter running. The human figures are mostly male and typically are drawn with such adornments as an elaborate head-dress, hairbelt, necklace, pendant tassels, armlets

Post-estuarine period. X-ray descriptive style. Wading bird. Koongarra area. (L.B.)

Post-estuarine period. X-ray descriptive style. Echidna. Deaf Adder. (I.J.M.)

and leg ornaments. They may carry a dilly bag, spear, boomerang, club, axe or stick. Females are usually portrayed unclothed and sometimes carrying objects such as a dilly bag, digging stick, spear and fire stick. In addition to the animals depicted in the earlier naturalistic drawings, the dynamic paintings include representations of other species, including long necked turtles and several bird and freshwater fish species. Creatures with human bodies and animal heads, apparently of flying foxes (bats), were also drawn. These animal-headed beings are the first examples of mythological painting in the rock art of Kakadu. Sometimes the people who drew the dynamic figures indicated sound, smells, animal tracks and emotions, such as pain, by a series of dashes. The complex compositions of this style, painted to suggest movement, predate by many thousands of years similar innovations in dynamic artistic expression elsewhere in the world.

The fourth art style of the pre-estuarine period, known as post-dynamic figures, shows even more stylised human beings. The figures are silhouettes and compared with previous paintings are grouped in relatively simple compositions with few animals and no animal-headed beings.

In a later style, called simple figures, people are depicted as one-line-thick, sticklike figures. They still wear head adornments and skirts and the males may carry boomerangs. The fighting pick is commonly carried by these people and is shown being used in fighting scenes.

Post-estuarine period. X-ray decorative style. Long necked turtle. Ubirr (Obiri Rock). (C.T.)

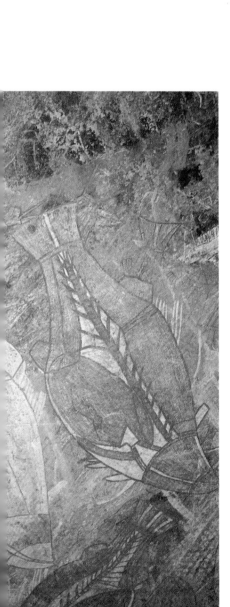

Post-estuarine period. X-ray descriptive style. Barramundi and eel tailed catfish. Ubirr (Obiri Rock). (C.T.)

The last style of the pre-estuarine period is represented by yam figures in which humans and certain animals are depicted with the outward shape of yam tubers. Vines and other appendages, possibly roots, trail from the yam figures. The animals depicted in this symbolic way are turtles, flying foxes and birds. This is the first known time when paintings of the mythological creature the rainbow serpent appear. Aboriginal religious beliefs associated with the rainbow snake are widespread in northern Australia and have been held for a very long time.

When the yam conceptual paintings were executed conditions had become wetter and sea levels were rising. As a consequence, less flat land would have been available to sustain the Aboriginal population and the moister climate would be more suitable for yams. Presumably, starch-filled yam tubers then became an important food for Aborigines.

Traditionally, a continuous supply of tubers is ensured by the harvesting practice. Yam tubers are carefully dug out of the ground using a digging stick and only the bottom portions are eaten. The knobbed heads are replanted and subsequently vines sprout from them. The vines grow above ground and twine around other plants in search of sunlight, the energy source for the manufacture of carbohydrates (starches and sugars) stored in the developing subterranean tuber. By harvesting and replanting in this way Aborigines could be certain of having a readily available food supply on their return to different places in their territories. This is an interesting early example of sustained use of a natural resource.

Estuarine period   The estuarine period of rock art began about 8000 years ago when, with further melting of the glacial sea, the sea level rose creating a broad salt marsh environment adjacent to the Arnhem Land Plateau. This environmental change is reflected in the artwork, favourite subjects being barramundi and, to a lesser extent, mullet, lesser salmon catfish and saltwater crocodiles. The mythical Lightning Man, Namargon, now appears in the paintings, presumably because intense electrical storms with much lightning occurred at this time.

A feature of the art of this period is its greater elaboration, with X-ray descriptive paintings displaying the internal organs and bone structures of animals. In some later drawings, stylised decorative patterns in various hatchings replace the more

Post-estuarine period. Fruit or edible tubers. Lightning Dreaming. (I.P.H.).

realistic anatomical representations. The previous, pre-estuarine period paintings are red with yellow or white sometimes used to emphasise outlines. The X-ray paintings of the estuarine period are different, the subject being first painted as a white silhouette on which anatomical details or patterns are superimposed in other colours.

Freshwater period   The freshwater period began about 1000 years ago when, as a result of ecological succession, the saline plains had been replaced in places by freshwater billabongs and paperbark swamps. As at present, these wetland areas would support flocks of geese and ducks and aquatic plants such as wild rice, water lilies and lotus lilies, all eaten by the Aboriginal people. This new wetland biota is depicted in the paintings, usually in the X-ray style. Hunters are also shown and often carry a goose wing fan.

Contact period This, the most recent art period, records the meetings of Aborigines with other people. It began in the sixteenth century when Macassan fishermen from Celebes came to the northern Australian coast to harvest trepang, a marine, slug-like animal much prized for culinary purposes in Asia. Centuries later, Europeans arrived on the scene, firstly explorers and then developers. Usually the Aboriginal artists depicted the newcomers accurately, but sometimes they failed to comprehend the new technology and rifles were drawn being used as though they were spears. Decorated hand stencils were also drawn and a new art form was introduced consisting of beeswax figures formed by pressing shaped pieces of wax on to rock faces.

Unfortunately, the Aboriginal population, having little immunity to introduced diseases, was decimated by epidemics of influenza, measles and leprosy. Many of the survivors moved to missions and settlements or were attracted to population centres, causing the traditional lands to be depopulated. In these circumstances, the contact period must have been catastrophic to Aboriginal people and placed great stress on them. The many sorcery paintings and casual paintings daubed on rock surfaces with fingers attest to the disturbing effects of the newcomers on Aboriginal society.

Guardians of paintings The tradition of painting on rock diminished at Kakadu as Aborigines were displaced from, or left, their clan territories during the cultural upheaval following the coming of Europeans. The elaborate and unusual blue paintings at Burrunguy (Nourlangie Rock) were painted as recently as 1964 but since then very little rock painting has been done at Kakadu. Aboriginal artists now produce paintings on pieces of bark from stringybark trees *Eucalyptus tetrodonta*, a practice which evolved from the decoration of the interiors of traditional wet season bark shelters. This art form is produced for sale and the paintings are often in the traditional style of rock art. Bark paintings represent a continuation of Aboriginal traditional painting and many are exhibited in the art galleries and museums of the world. Nevertheless, Aboriginal interest in the rock paintings remains strong. The traditional Aboriginal inheritors and guardians of the art sites live within the Park and individual Aborigines have responsibility for the care and protection of specific rock art work.

This unique and ancient cultural heritage of art must be preserved as a vital, living force. Aboriginal people are anxious to ensure that the legends and stories illustrated by the paintings, and as passed down and interpreted to them by their forebears, are remembered by future generations. Whilst some are secret to Aborigines, others can be told to visitors to the Park without danger to the teller. The Australian National Parks and Wildlife Service is working closely with the Aboriginal guardians to protect the paintings and to make some available for visitors to see. Discretion needs to be employed in providing access to, or information on, certain art sites, especially where the sites are regarded by Aborigines as sacred or of a dangerous nature. Not all art sites are accessible but the artwork on display at Ubirr (Obiri Rock) and Burrunguy (Nourlangie Rock) covers a wide range of styles.

Post-estuarine period. Female with yams in dilly bags. Cannon Hill. (I.P.H.)

Post-estuarine period. Mythical being. Koongarra area. (C.T.)

37

Post-estuarine period. Sorcery
painting. (C.T.)

Post-estuarine period. X-ray
descriptive style. Eel tailed catfish.
East Alligator. (I.J.M.)

Many individual rock paintings and compositions are of great
beauty and the rock art of Kakadu compares favourably with the
much publicised palaeolithic cave paintings of western Europe.
The artwork is remarkable for the completeness of the story it
unfolds of human settlement and resource use during the great
physical and climatic changes following the last glaciation. It also
provides an illuminating insight into the evolution of artistic
styles and beliefs. Probably no other national park has such a rich
cultural heritage of proved antiquity and with the descendants of
the original people living in it and actively participating in its
management. The preservation of this heritage and its
meaningful interpretation are of prime importance for park
management. Both must be achieved with the agreement and
co-operation of Aboriginal people.

Contemporary Aboriginal culture The Aboriginal people of
Kakadu were grouped into at least nine clans and there were
several distinct languages. Unfortunately, some languages have
fallen, or are falling, into disuse. For example, Gagadju is now
only spoken by a few people and the major languages used in the
area are Gunwinggu, Gundjeibmi, English and its derivative
Kriol. With the decline of the clan system and the loss of
Aboriginal languages, it is easy to overlook the contemporary
cultural life of the Aboriginal people and the significance of the
bonds linking them with their clan estates.

Before Europeans came to Kakadu, probably about 2000
Aboriginal people lived in the area, their numbers and lifestyles
being determined by its natural resources. The number
decreased greatly following the arrival of Europeans and, at the
time of proclamation, only about fifty Aborigines lived

Post-estuarine period. X-ray decorative style. Brush tailed wallaby. Ubirr (Obiri Rock). (C.T.)

Post-esturine period. X-ray decorative style. Wallaby. Malakunanydja. (I.J.M.)

permanently in the Park. Following proclamation, Aboriginal people are returning in substantial numbers and increasingly are participating effectively in park management. Approximately 250 Aborigines now live in Kakadu grouped in a number of small communities. Some 800 other Aboriginal people live in neighbouring townships such as Oenpelli and at outstations in western Arnhem Land. They visit the Park regularly and take a great interest in what is happening there.

The social aspects of Aboriginal culture are often difficult for non-Aboriginal people to understand. Essentially they are based on the belief that Aboriginal people are part of the land and without it have no physical or spiritual security. There is a complex system of kinship relationships and of clan (Gunmugurrgurr) membership. Membership of a clan derives from the father and gives rights of interest and control over what happens in the clan estate. The significance attached to traditional social relationships in day to day life is an expression of the strength of Aboriginal culture in the Park. By clan membership and the attendant attachment to land, individual Aborigines have been recognised as traditional owners of the land under European law. Under Aboriginal customs and law the issue was never in doubt. In the management of Kakadu National Park great importance is attached to recognition of Aboriginal ownership and to ensuring, so far as possible, that Aborigines there continue to live the lifestyle they feel most comfortable with.

Whilst Aborigines choose to adopt some benefits of European society, they still attach great importance to the pursuit of Aboriginal interests. Belief in the dreamtime, the creation period and the mythical forces associated with it continue to be of special relevance to Aboriginal people. Secret ceremonies to introduce young people to Aboriginal religous life continue in western Arnhem Land, as does the passing on of legends describing the reasons for things being as they are. Hunting and the gathering of plant material afford opportunities for the elders to pass to Aboriginal children knowledge of the land and the cultural heritage. These activities, by involving travel, also enable checks to be made that all is well with their estates.

Non-Aboriginal settlement   Visitors to the Park are often interested to learn about people, other than Aborigines, who came to the area and how they lived. The coastal Aborigines had

Post-estuarine contact period. Sailing ship with anchor chain and dinghy. Burrunguy (Nourlangie Rock). (I.J.M.)

Post-estuarine contact period. Figure made by pressing beeswax pellets on rock surface. East Alligator. (I.J.M.)

a long association with the Macassans, who for centuries sailed to northern Australia in their praus, a kind of sailing ship. They sailed southwards mainly from the island of Celebes using the north-west monsoon winds and stayed for half a year before returning home with their lucrative cargo of trepang on the south-east trade winds. The harvesting of trepang was a large scale operation; Flinders reports that in 1803 sixty praus carrying 1000 men were engaged in harvesting trepang. About 10 tonnes of trepang were taken by each prau. Pearlshell, turtleshell, shark fins, sandalwood and wood of cypress pine were also harvested.

Aborigines were attracted to the camps where trepang and other products were processed for export and Aborigines may have visited the home ports of the Macassans. Unfortunately, comparatively little is known of the relationships between Aborigines and Macassans, but some Aborigines may have some Macassan ancestry. Aboriginal languages and place names provide evidence of the long association with Macassans. Numerous Macassan words were adopted by the coastal Aborigines, especially words to do with sailing, but now these are not used much. Words which reflect this contact and still used in Aboriginal languages along the Arnhem Land coast include balanda for Europeans (from the Malay word for the Dutch), rupiah for money, djurra for paper and lippa lippa for dugout canoes. When the praus were prohibited from the northern coastal waters early this century, this long contact with the Macassans was broken.

Post-estuarine contact period. Explorer or stockman on horse. East Alligator. (I.J.M)

More is known of the Europeans who came to Kakadu for various reasons. A Dutch vessel, after which Arnhem Land is named, surveyed the northern coast in 1644. Captain Phillip Parker King was instructed by the British government to chart the northern coastline, including Van Diemen Gulf, and in so doing sailed up most of the river estuaries in 1818. King gave the East, West and South Alligator Rivers their names, reportedly in the mistaken belief that the many crocodiles sighted were alligators. Detailed surveys of the three Alligator Rivers were carried out in 1885 by Commander J. Carrington, who commented on the many buffaloes seen.

The first explorer to cross the area by land was a dropout medical student, Ludwig Leichhardt, whose expedition was financed by friends. He entered the Park area in 1845 and recorded in his journal impressions of the scenery and descriptions of the new plant and animal species he discovered. Several of these species, such as different kinds of grevilleas and melaleucas and a grasshopper, have been rediscovered only recently by scientists. Leichhardt commented on the great variety and abundance of birds and that the many groups of Aborigines he met were friendly. He described the valley of the South Alligator River as most magnificently grassed and full of swamps and billabongs.

Leichhardt was followed in 1866 by the explorer John McKinlay, who was much less perceptive. McKinlay, financed by the South Australian Government, which was then responsible for the Northern Territory, had been instructed to seek a new capital for the Territory. He and his large party travelled with great difficulty across the area. They considered it to be inhospitable and regarded the Aborigines they encountered as inferior and degenerate people.

Subsequently, other explorers, gold fossickers, buffalo shooters, crocodile hunters, cattlemen, timber gatherers (cypress pine was the commercial species), safari operators, mineral prospectors, miners, commercial and sports fishermen, missionaries, scientists, tourists and park managers came to the area. All used, and some abused, the area. Inevitably any industries set up were on a small scale and controlled by Europeans, with Aborigines employed as manual workers. Since the industries normally relied on the exploitation of natural resources, they usually proved to be temporary, but all left their mark and to varying degrees disrupted Aboriginal society.

Aboriginal people were the first to exploit the mineral resources and for thousands of years gathered rocks on the ground to make stone tools and pigments for their paintings. European explorers found traces of gold in the headwaters of the Mary River in 1870 and the Pine Creek goldfield was discovered a year later. The gold discoveries precipitated a rush of prospectors, who employed Aborigines in their search for minerals. Only minor gold deposits were located; some were worked by Chinese mining teams in the latter part of the nineteenth century. The returns from gold mining were poor and the deposits of copper and tin discovered proved uneconomic and consequently mining waned.

More recently, the confirmation of uranium deposits at Coronation Hill and El Sharana in the upper South Alligator basin rekindled mining interest. Using more sophisticated exploration techniques, three major uranium deposits were discovered, namely Ranger, Jabiluka and Koongarra. Following the Ranger Uranium Environmental Inquiry, production of uranium commenced at the Ranger Mine in 1980, with various safeguards in relation to possible impacts of uranium mining on the environment and Aboriginal society. Relatively large numbers of construction workers and later mine operators and their families have been brought into the Region. The recreational activities of many of these are centred on the Park. Royalties gained from mining are enabling Aboriginal investment and participation in the development of tourism in the Park to provide an assured long-term income.

Post-estuarine contact period. Blue paintings drawn by Najombolmi (Barramundi Charlie) in mid 1960s. Burrunguy (Nourlangie Rock). (C.T.)

The history of the Macassan sailors and almost two centuries of European involvement in Kakadu is part of the story of the opening up of northern Australia and the impact on an ancient Aboriginal culture. However, few Macassans or Europeans successfully came to terms with the isolation and hazardous environmental conditions and permanently settled there. In contrast, Aboriginal people have occupied the area for thousands of years sustained by their traditional customs and culture. Their occupation gained strength from the experience of many previous generations, so that progressively they came to understand and effectively use the environment. Far from being an untamed wilderness, Kakadu has a long and fascinating history of human occupation and cultural evolution.

Post-estuarine contact period. X-ray style blue painting by Najombolmi (Barramundi Charlie). Burrunguy (Nourlangie Rock). (M.H.)

43

A HERITAGE OF AUSTRALIAN ANIMALS AND PLANTS

Conservation status   Australia is an island continent and as a consequence, except for migratory species, Australian animals and plants have evolved in isolation and many are specific to the continent. However, numerous Kakadu species have retained affinities with those of South-East Asia, the nearest land mass, apparently reflecting their shared common ancestry when Australia and Asia were joined together.

Kakadu is the home of a rich heritage of native animals and plants; many are both attractive and of scientific interest. Because of the value of native animals and plants to Aborigines, it is not surprising that they feature in Aboriginal mythology and rock art. The rock paintings, particularly of animals, provide evidence both of long-term changes in the species present and of the continued presence in the area of other species for thousands of years.

Each of the numerous Park habitats has its own characteristic community of living things interacting in innumerable ways with one another and with their environments. Knowledge of these functional relationships is critical for management of the Park. Detailed research is providing vital information to enable the implementation of effective management practices to safeguard this remarkable range of species and habitats. Both are irreplaceable, having resulted from over 20 million years of evolution.

The species present at Kakadu differ greatly in distribution and conservation status. Some are common in Australia or across tropical northern Australia and are not under threat. Other species though widespread in northern Australia are rare and

Dingoes were brought to Australia by Aborigines thousands of years ago. (I.J.M.)

Leichhardt's grasshoppers restricted to a few species of aromatic shrubs. (M.P.)

45

their survival may depend in large measure on the protection afforded by the National Park. A few species have a very restricted distribution, being found only at Kakadu and sometimes only in certain localities because of their very precise environmental requirements. Knowledge of the abundance and distribution of species in the Park helps to ensure the protection of rare and endangered species and improves the likelihood of people seeing plants and animals of special interest to them.

All the different kinds of native living things present have a role to play in maintaining the delicate harmony of Kakadu with its self-regulating and continuing sequence of reproduction, life, death and decay. Of all tropical wilderness areas in the southern hemisphere Kakadu National Park is the most outstanding

Northern brushtail possum resting. (I.J.M.)

sanctuary, providing a haven where a wide variety of animals and plants, including some rare or endangered species, can survive in natural surroundings. Let us keep it that way.

■

Animals   Whilst Kakadu is renowned for its variety of wild animals, undoubtedly the species tally is incomplete. Already scientists have recorded about 50 mammal, 275 bird, 75 reptile, 25 frog and 55 fish species. There is a great diversity of insects; about 4500 species have been recognised. As systematic faunal surveys of different habitats are completed, new species for the Park, and some new to science, are being discovered and species not seen for many years are being rediscovered.

Most native animals at Kakadu are harmless to people but some can be plain annoying, especially insects which buzz around, bite or suck blood from people. Mosquitoes thrive in the

Kakadu environment and can be particularly troublesome to campers. Other creatures such as venomous snakes and large crocodiles are dangerous if provoked. Animals protected in national parks tend to have little fear of people and, with some justification, may regard people as food or as intruders to their territories, posing a challenging threat to themselves or their offspring. Naturally, in these circumstances some wild animals may react aggressively to humans. Consequently it is advisable not to act foolishly by taking risks. Watching wild animals at Kakadu can be a pleasant experience but sensible people keep a safe distance from wild animals and use telephoto lenses to take close-up photographs. Most native animals are nocturnal and the best time to see some species is dusk or shortly after dawn.

The northern quoll (native cat), a fierce carnivore. (I.J.M.)

Mammals The native mammals are generally shy and avoid people by hiding or running away. Dingoes or wild dogs *Canis familiaris dingo* range widely in the Park, feeding mainly on other mammals, birds and reptiles. Most often they are encountered as single animals or as a pair but sometimes family packs of up to five are seen. Virtually all dingoes at Kakadu are pure bred for there has been little interbreeding with domestic dogs.

Macropods are common in some habitats. The gregarious agile wallabies *Macropus agilis* often move in groups through the open woodland whilst wallaroos or euros *M. robustus* are usually seen as solitary animals in upland wooded areas. Mobs of antilopine kangaroos *M. antilopinus* are occasionally seen on stony ridges or

Pouch with six young of northern quoll. (I.J.M.)

47

The sandstone antechinus discovered in 1948 occurs only on the escarpment. (I.J.M.)

Water rat feasting on fish. (I.J.M.)

Antilopine kangaroo. (I.J.M.)

in open woodland, particularly where plants are regenerating after fire. Spectacled hare wallabies *Lagorchestes conspicillatus* and northern nailtail wallabies *Onychogalea unguifera* are present in small numbers in grassland and open woodland areas. The very shy black wallaroos *Macropus bernardus* are largely confined to the Park. The relatively small nabarleks *Peradorcas concinna* and short eared rock wallabies *Petrogale brachyotis* inhabit the rocky formations of the escarpment and outliers.

The smaller mammals tend to be inconspicuous and only seen briefly. The arboreal sugar gliders *Petaurus breviceps* and northern brushtail possums *Trichosurus arnhemensis* as well as northern brown bandicoots *Isoodon macrourus* are sometimes observed during the day in wooded areas. Several kinds of water rats and other small rodents live in freshwater lagoon and floodplain habitats but are rarely encountered. Echidnas *Tachyglossus aculeatus*, sometimes called spiny anteaters, are to be found on the escarpment. Some small mammals are largely confined to rocky areas; typical of these are rock possums *Pseudocheirus dahli*, Woodward's thick tailed rats *Zyzomys woodwardi* and Harney's marsupial mice *Parantechinus bilarni*, only known since 1948. Many species of small mammals are essentially nocturnal and are aggressive, fierce carnivores, for instance northern native cats or northern quolls *Dasyurus hallucatus* and arboreal phascogales *Phascogale tapoatafa*.

Within the Park there is a remarkable variety of flying mammals, twenty-six of the sixty-five species of Australian bats being present. The bats of Kakadu range in size from large, fruit-eating flying foxes, weighing at maturity over half a kilogram, to small, mouse-sized animals. Whilst some people are apprehensive of bats, the ill repute of bats is undeserved. These remarkable animals are highly adapted to enable them to fly and navigate at night. Bats spend the days roosting in groves of trees, caves, rock overhangs, tree hollows and under bark. They are often seen flying at dusk when they leave their roosts to forage.

The two species of flying foxes present at Kakadu, black flying foxes *Pteropus alecto* and little red flying foxes *P. scapulatus*, are the most conspicuous of the bats. Roosting by day in large, and somewhat smelly, camps in mangroves, paperbark swamps and monsoon forests, they emerge in droves to feed at night on the fruits, flowers and leaves of trees, particularly of *Ficus*, *Eucalyptus* and *Melaleuca* species. Often they are seen, or heard, squabbling

48

amongst themselves whilst feeding at Nourlangie Camp and Park Headquarters. Since flying foxes are important pollinators of plants and disperse viable seed through their excrement, they are important for the perpetuation of some plant species.

Kakadu is a key refuge for at least four species of endangered bats: ghost bats *Macroderma gigas*, orange horseshoe bats *Rhinonicteris aurantius*, lesser wart nosed horseshoe bats *Hipposideros stenotis* and white striped sheathtail bats *Taphozous kapalgensis*.

Ghost bats are carnivorous, feeding on insects, mammals, small birds, and even other bats on occasion. They roost in caves and overhangs with stable temperature and humidity regimes. Orange horseshoe bats are very rare, with possibly fewer than

Ghost bats are efficient night flyers. (G.B.B.)

2000 living in Australia. Although individuals have been seen at Kakadu, no roosting sites have been discovered. Bats of this species are known to roost in very hot, humid caves and being very sensitive to human interference may abandon caves if disturbed. They feed on moths, beetles, wasps and ants caught while flying low over the ground. Little is known of the biology of lesser wart nosed horseshoe bats. They have two warty protuberances on the nose which may aid echo location of objects when flying at night. White striped sheathtail bats, only discovered in 1979, are apparently endemic to Kakadu National Park. Found in open eucalypt and pandanus woodland, they fly high and fast in pursuit of insects and are believed to roost in the hollows of trees or under exfoliating bark.

Northern blossom bats feed on nectar and in so doing pollinate plants. (I.J.M.)

The jabiru stork, Australia's only stork, is wary of people. (I.J.M.)

Birds Kakadu National Park has a remarkable combination of bird species; about a third of all Australian species has been recorded there. In particular, it is a major Australian refuge for many kinds of tropical birds.

Birds of prey range widely over the Park, differing in size from large, majestic wedgetailed eagles *Aquila audax* to small, but lightning quick, collared sparrowhawks *Accipiter cirrhocephalus*. Black kites *Milvus migrans* are the most common birds of prey in the Park. Possibly the most frequent bird sound heard in the dry season is the shrill cry of the ubiquitous whistling kites *Haliastur sphenurus*, gliding gracefully or circling on thermal air currents on the look-out for carrion. Letter winged kites *Elanus scriptus*, a relatively rare species, are present in the Park and are most active at night, when they may be seen hunting over the floodplains for rodents. The discovery of a small breeding population at Kakadu extended the previously known range in the Northern Territory by several hundred kilometres. Both grey and white phases of grey goshawks *Accipiter novaehollandiae* occur in wooded areas. Rare red goshawks *Erythrotriorchis radiatus*, which feed mainly on other birds, are largely restricted to the sandstone woodland. White breasted sea eagles *Haliaeetus leucogaster* are often seen singly or in pairs perched on trees overlooking billabongs or flying with strong, leisurely wing beats along waterways in search of unsuspecting fish on which they swoop and catch them in their talons.

Along the coast and on the tidal flats there is a great variety of birds. Some are all year residents, others are migratory, mainly

Successful strike by a white breasted sea eagle. (I.J.M.)

Water whistling ducks rarely leave the water. (I.J.M.)

Spotless crake. (I.J.M.)

Magpie geese and young. (I.J.M.)

returning from more northerly or southerly latitudes at the onset of the wet or the dry season. The coastal bird fauna includes boobies, cormorants, curlews, egrets, greenshanks, herons, ospreys, oyster catchers, plovers, rails, stilts, sandpipers, terns and turnstones.

The mangrove swamps are important roosting and breeding sites for many bird species, including colonial nesters such as egrets and cormorants. Some birds are largely confined to the mangroves. Examples of these are mangrove kingfishers *Halycon chloris*, mangrove robins *Eopsaltria pulverulenta*, chestnut rails *Eulabeornis castaneoventris*, white breasted whistlers *Pachycephala lanioides*, yellow white eyes *Zosterops lutea*, large billed warblers *Gerygone magnirostris* and mangrove warblers *G. levigaster*. Mangrove warblers are noteworthy for their sustained sweet song and compact pear-shaped nests, made of bark, grass stems and seaweed neatly bound together with spider web, and usually seen suspended from leafy mangrove branches.

Because of their variety and profusion much interest has centred on waterbirds. At nesting time the breeding grounds, hidden amidst the dense sedge and grass cover of the floodplains, resound with the noise of geese and ducks. The populations of some waterbird species, although abundant in Kakadu, are largely restricted in Australia to a narrow band along the northern coastline. Typical of these are magpie geese *Anseranas semipalmata*, green pygmy geese *Nettapus pulchellus*, Burdekin ducks or Radjah shelducks *Tadorna radjah* and water whistling ducks *Dendrocygna arcuata*.

Some waterbirds common at Kakadu are relatively widespread in Australia, for instance jabiru storks *Xenorhynchus asiaticus*, the namesake of Jabiru town with enormous spear-like beaks to catch fish, and lotus birds or lilytrotters *Irediparra gallinacea*, whose long hind toes enable them to walk on water weeds and which build their nests on floating vegetation. Other widespread species include pelicans *Pelecanus conspicillatus* and darters *Anhinga melanogaster*, sometimes called snake birds because of their resemblance to snakes when swimming submerged with the head and neck above water. Cormorants, egrets, herons and ibis abound. Nankeen or rufous night herons *Nycticorax caledonicus* are very common along the watercourses. Recently a large rookery of this heron, with as many as 2000 nesting birds, was discovered in rainforest at Kakadu. This is the only known rookery of the species in the Northern Territory. Brolgas *Grus rubicundus*, noted for their graceful, elaborate, ballet-like courtship dance, are plentiful at some places in the Park.

Throughout the world tropical freshwater bodies and swamps are being drained and reclaimed for agriculture so that the protection of the remainder is becoming ever more critical for the conservation of waterbirds. The wetlands of Kakadu support such a large number and diversity of waterbirds that the Park is probably the most important tropical waterbird reserve.

The tree-lined margins of the inland waters provide food and shelter for myriads of colourful birds. Here can be seen six kinds of kingfishers, including little kingfishers *Ceyx pusillus*, Australia's smallest kingfisher, blue winged kookaburras *Dacelo leachii*, rainbow bee eaters *Merops ornatus* and several species of

A busy egret rookery in mangroves.
(G.L.M.)

51

flycatchers. When the paperbark trees of the floodplain swamps are in flower nectar is plentiful and many nectar-feeding birds such as honeyeaters and lorikeets are attracted to the paperbarks.

Birds are less abundant away from water and the avifauna of the drier grassland, woodland and rocky areas, though rich in species, is very different from that of the wetlands. Large birds such as bustards *Ardeotis australis* and emus *Dromaius novaehollandiae* are present but rarely seen. Parrots are well represented and flocks of red collared lorikeets *Trichoglossus rubritorquis* or of varied lorikeets *Psitteuteles versicolor* chatter noisily in their constant search for nectar among the flowering trees. The relatively rare northern rosella parrots *Platycercus venustus* occur in open woodland and along the escarpment and

The white ibis constantly probes the mud in search of insects, snails and frogs. (L.B.)

Great bower bird at bower decorated with shells. (I.J.M.)

Varied lorikeets chatter noisily as they feed on tree nectar and pollen. (G.L.M.)

52

plateau. Hooded parrots *Psephotus dissimilis*, classified as endangered, have been sighted in the Park and it is hoped that their numbers will increase with careful management. Noisy groups of red tailed black cockatoos *Calyptorhynchus magnificus* can be observed particularly in recently burnt areas foraging for cracked seeds. Sulphur crested cockatoos *Cacatua galerita* and red winged parrots *Aprosmictus erythropterus* are commonly seen or heard in savannah woodland habitats. Several dove species are present including peaceful doves *Geopelia striata*, bar shouldered doves *G. humeralis* and diamond doves *G. cuneata*. Other bird species of the drier areas include owls, tawny frogmouths *Podargus strigoides*, owlet nightjars *Aegotheles cristatus*, nightjars and cuckoos. Characteristically, the cuckoos are parasitic, laying their

The spotted nightjar is well camouflaged. (G.L.M.)

eggs in the nests of other birds which become foster parents to the hatchling cuckoos. Occasionally, the decorated bowers of great bower birds *Chlamydera nuchalis* are discovered on the forest floor. Incubation mounds of scrub fowls *Megapodius freycinet* are abundant in some areas of the coastal monsoon rainforest.

A few bird species unique to the Kakadu region are largely restricted to the escarpment and its outliers, particularly the deep rock gorges and forested gullies. Though locally fairly common they are rarely observed. Such endemics are banded pigeons *Ptilinopus cinctus* and chestnut quilled rock pigeons *Petrophassa rufipennis*, which may be seen at Burrunguy (Nourlangie Rock). Rare white throated grass wrens *Amytornis woodwardi* and lavender flanked wrens *Malurus lamberti dulcis* inhabit the open scrub spinifex community of the sandstone.

Grass owl hunting. (I.J.M.)

53

The giant cave gecko, a night hunter. (I.J.M.)

A brightly coloured male skink. (I.J.M.)

Reptiles Australia possesses a very rich and varied range of reptiles and Kakadu has representatives of all major Australian groups. The reptiles of Kakadu are well adapted to survive in an environment of constantly high temperatures and extreme seasonal moisture differences.

Small skinks occur in many habitats but are most abundant in woodland areas. Often brightly coloured with complex spotted and striped patterns, skinks are readily noticeable as they forage energetically for insects amongst leaf litter on the forest floor, on tree trunks or between rocks. Clear membranes fused over the eyes of some species are believed to limit water loss. Arnhem Land skinks *Ctenotus arnhemensis*, first described in 1981, are restricted to the sandstone massifs and gorges of the western Arnhem Land escarpment.

Less obvious than the skinks are the geckoes, which are essentially nocturnal. Some species have foot pads and large eyes, enabling them to climb vertical surfaces and catch insects at night. Geckoes are often seen hunting or resting on tree trunks and on the walls and ceilings of buildings or hiding in cracks or fissures in the sandstone rocks. Giant cave geckoes *Pseudothecadactylus lindneri* are restricted to a few caves and fissures of the stony escarpment country. They emerge in the evening in search of insects, spiders and other geckoes to eat. Recently a previously unknown ground-dwelling gecko species *Diplodactylus occultus* has been discovered in the eucalypt forest of Kakadu.

Several lizard species may be seen at Kakadu. Individuals of the northern race of eastern blue tongued lizards *Tiliqua scincoides intermedia* are sometimes sighted in wooded areas, especially

54

immediately after the early wet season rainstorms. Several kinds of dragon lizards are present including chameleon dragons *Chelosania brunnea*, two lined dragons *Diporiphora bilineata* and Gilbert's dragons *Lophognathus gilberti*. The spectacular frilled lizards *Chlamydosaurus kingii*, the largest of the dragon lizards, occur in forests and open woodlands. They may be seen at the onset of the wet season after leaving hollow logs and branches where they sheltered during the dry. When alarmed, they extend the brightly coloured membraneous frill around their necks before retreating at a fast pace up nearby trees. Frilled lizards are unusual in being bipedal, running on their two hind legs. Larger lizards present, some over 1 metre long, include the relatively ubiquitous Gould's goannas *Varanus gouldii*, sand goannas

The frilled lizard seeks escape up a tree. (I.J.M.)

Blue tongued lizard. (I.J.M.)

V. panoptes of the sedgelands, arboreal spotted monitors *V. timorensis* on tree trunks, mangrove monitors *V. indicus* in mangrove swamps and Mitchell's water monitors *V. mitchelli* and Merten's water monitors *V. mertensi* in freshwater habitats. Occasionally these large reptiles, particularly Gould's and the floodplain goannas, are encountered on road verges or on the banks of billabongs. Goannas are regarded as good tucker by Aborigines.

Many kinds of snakes, both venomous and non-venomous, occur in the Park. Although few people see a snake during their visit to Kakadu, snakes are common in some habitats, particularly floodplains, woodland margins, monsoon forests and the escarpment country. In the monsoon forests they often

Merten's water monitor on a fishing expedition. (I.J.M.)

The dangerous king brown snake may be 2 metres long. (G.L.M.)

The death adder is a superb predator. (I.J.M.)

Oenpelli pythons recently recognised by scientists but long known to Aborigines as Nawarran. (I.J.M.)

live near or between the aerial roots of banyan figs *Ficus virens*. Some poisonous snakes have been found in staff houses and as a precaution the Park staff clear the vegetation and burn off dead leaves and branches around their houses to reduce the likelihood of having snakes as unwelcome guests.

Three highly venomous snake species in the Park are taipans *Oxyuranus scutellatus*, one of Australia's large and dangerous snakes, king brown snakes *Pseudechis australis* and northern death adders *Acanthophis praelongus*. Northern death adders usually hide in the soil or leaf litter and attract their prey of small animals to them by twitching their tails as a lure. If approached by people, they do not retreat like most other snakes but remain motionless and may strike with lightning speed. Persons walking at night, when death adders are most active, should wear stout boots and use a flashlight.

The fish-eating, non-venomous aquatic file snakes *Acrochordus arafurae* are common in freshwater areas and are eaten by Aborigines. Pythons are fairly common in the Park. Water pythons *Liasis fuscus* hunt birds and rats on the sedgeland and other wet habitats and at bird nesting times feast on eggs, especially those of magpie geese *Anseranas semipalmata*. Olive pythons *L. olivaceus*, children's pythons *L. childreni* and black headed pythons *Aspidites melanocephalus* are woodland species and occasionally may be seen crossing park roads. Oenpelli pythons *Morelia oenpelliensis*, discovered in 1977 in the rocky escarpment country, are attractive large snakes. They seem harmless to people and apparently are endemic to the escarpment of the Kakadu area. Sea snakes and rear fanged mangrove snakes are occasionally found in coastal tidal waters.

57

A female flatback turtle digs her nest in beach sand. (I.J.M.)

At least five kinds of freshwater turtles inhabit the rivers, rockpools and swamplands of the Park. The species most often seen are northern snake necked turtles *Chelodina rugosa* and herbivorous snapping turtles *Elseya dentata*. The rarer pitted shelled turtles known locally as pig nosed turtles *Carettochelys insculpta* are more secretive and prefer to hide between pandanus roots or among thick waterside vegetation. These large turtles, discovered in Kakadu in 1973, were previously thought to be confined to southern New Guinea. Marine turtles, including flatback turtles *Chelonia depressa*, green turtles *C. mydas*, hawksbill turtles *Eretmochelys imbricata* and Pacific Ridley turtles *Lepidochelys olivacea*, frequent the coastal waters off Kakadu. Being protected in the Park they nest on the beaches in comparative safety,

Pig nosed turtles first discovered in Australia in 1973 at Kakadu. (G.L.M.)

although goannas and other natural predators take turtle eggs from the nests and prey on hatchling turtles during their perilous journey from the nest to the sea.

Both species of Australian crocodiles occur in Kakadu. As the largest carnivorous animals in the Park, crocodiles help to regulate the numbers of other animals and so maintain a natural balance between species and the aquatic environment. The crocodile populations are heavily depleted throughout their natural range after many years of exploitative harvesting. Under the existing management regime in the Park, they are recovering in numbers and larger animals are more abundant. During the cooler, dry months crocodiles can be seen sunning on the banks of rivers and billabongs.

Freshwater crocodiles *Crocodylus johnstoni* are identified by their long slender snouts and rarely attain more than 3 metres in length. Relatively harmless to humans, they feed on fish, frogs and other small animals and are most common in upland rivers and billabongs fringed with extensive sand bars and pandanus trees. In contrast, estuarine or saltwater crocodiles *C. porosus* have broad snouts. Though most abundant in the tidal rivers, coastal swamps, mangroves and billabongs of the floodplains, they are also present in freshwater billabongs far from the coast. Mature animals may be over 5 metres long. Occasionally large saltwater crocodiles venture upstream where they live in small creeks at the escarpment base. Apparently these are mainly old bulls evicted from their former territories and leading a solitary bachelor life.

Northern snake necked turtle. (G.L.M.)

Flatback turtle hatchlings make a dash for the sea. Only mature females return to land. (I.J.M.)

Freshwater crocodiles are identified by their narrow snouts. (R.W.G.J.)

Crocodiles reproduce by laying eggs. The female freshwater crocodile excavates a chamber in sand in which are laid about fifteen eggs in the middle of the dry season. The female saltwater crocodile lays its eggs in a nest, about a metre high, made of soil and vegetation on the banks of rivers and swamps and sometimes on floating vegetation mats. About fifty eggs may be laid in a nest but many are destroyed by the rising floodwaters and some are taken by predators such as goannas and wild pigs. Heat generated by the decomposition of the organic matter in the nests of saltwater crocodiles is thought to assist incubation. Apparently nest temperature affects the sex of the hatchlings; generally for saltwater crocodiles higher temperatures give a greater proportion of males whilst the opposite is true for

freshwater crocodiles. Crocodile eggs hatch about ten to twelve weeks after laying. Before hatching, young crocodiles call from inside the eggs, causing the mother to excavate the nest to facilitate their escape. During incubation female saltwater crocodiles only rarely leave the vicinity of their nests and defend them against intruders. Female freshwater crocodiles stay in the vicinity of their nests but generally are less aggressive.

Unlike the relatively inoffensive freshwater crocodiles, saltwater crocodiles will attack large animals such as dogs and buffaloes, people and sometimes even the outboard motors of boats. Large crocodiles are a tourist attraction but their presence means it is dangerous for people to go into waterbodies in the Park. Where an individual crocodile is troublesome and poses a

Saltwater or estuarine crocodiles over 5 metres long may be seen on sandbanks. (I.J.M.)

public threat there is pressure to kill or capture it. Residential crocodiles have distinct territories and may exhibit a well-developed homing instinct. This territorial attachment creates a problem because captured crocodiles translocated elsewhere in the Park may return to their home territory.

■

Amphibians   The amphibian fauna of the Park is highly adapted to the marked climatic extremes of drought and floods. During the dry season frogs are rarely seen. Many are then dormant and aestivate in the soil, hollow limbs of trees or rock crevices to await the onset of the wet season. The large, flat headed frogs *Cyclorana australis*, for instance, live in burrows in the ground during the dry and only come out once the wet

A male green tree frog inflates its throat to call for a mate. (I.J.M.)

Frogs emerge from their burrows at the onset of the rains. (I.J.M.)

A male northern spadefoot toad assumes grotesque proportions as it makes its mating call. (I.J.M.)

begins. The males then congregate around billabongs and water-filled buffalo wallows to form breeding choruses attracting the females by their noise.

Frogs only become conspicuous at Kakadu during the wet season, when the billabongs, swamps and roadside ditches are filled with water. At this time frogs and tadpoles have available a plentiful supply of food, such as algae, vegetation, insects, dragonfly nymphs and other tadpoles.

Frogs depend on standing water for reproduction and consequently breeding occurs in the wet. The bush then becomes alive with a crescendo of noise from the chorusing male frogs, each species having its own characteristic call. Floating vegetation often provides a calling or feeding platform.

Frogs rely on camouflage to avoid discovery. (I.J.M.)

Temporary waterbodies may be crammed during the wet season with large breeding colonies of frogs and their offspring. The frogs of some species are opportunistic breeders and, if rain falls in the dry season, attempt to breed. For instance, after rain *Uperoleia inundata* emerges from the damp soil and the booming call of the green tree frog *Litoria caerulea* can be heard from hollows in tree trunks.

Frogs are most abundant in swamps and sedgeland and along the margins of billabongs and freshwater pools. They avoid saline habitats. The relatively few species recorded in the coastal mangrove forests include the green tree frog *Litoria bicolor* and the marbled frog *Limnodynastes convexiusculus*. Most kinds of frogs are restricted to particular habitats. Carpenter frogs *Megistolotis lignarius* are known only from the sandstone hills and gorges of the escarpment. Here other frog species of restricted distribution are also found, for instance saxicoline tree frogs *Litoria coplandi* and the small frogs *L. meiriana* common in waterholes on the escarpment. Other frogs live in the wet leaf litter of swampy areas; typical of these are the tiny dwarf rocket frogs *L. dorsalis*. The frogs *L. dahli* may be abundant in deep, flooded depressions where they float with outstretched legs and only their eyes protruding above the water surface. Powerful swimmers, they are active predators on insects and other frogs, including their own kind.

The multitude of frogs produced in the wet season constitutes a major food source for other animals. Wading birds, kingfishers,

Small frogs are eaten by larger frogs. (I.J.M.)

fish, snakes and other reptiles feast on the tadpoles and frogs abounding in the waterbodies. Most frogs rely on camouflage as a protection against predators, their multicoloured skins blending with the background. By changing the shape of dark skin cells the skin colour can be adjusted to some degree. In contrast, juveniles of ground dwelling spadefoot toads *Notaden melanoscaphus* have a striking, colourful appearance. This is thought to warn predators of their toxicity since glandular secretions from the toad skins are poisonous.

Fish   The first comprehensive scientific survey of the fish fauna of Kakadu dates back to 1948 and possibly more is known of the fish of the Park than of any other animal group. The large

The male saxicoline tree frog rides on the female ready to fertilise the eggs. (I.J.M.)

number of fish paintings in Aboriginal rock art emphasises the great importance of fish to them and this interest has been reinforced more recently by the activities of commercial and recreational fishermen. With the growth of mining activities, researchers have investigated the possibility of using fish to indicate any changes in water properties resulting from large scale uranium mining.

Some marine fish occur in the tidal reaches of the rivers and river whaler sharks *Carcharhinus leucas*, sawfish *Pristis microdon* and stingrays *Dasyatis* species may penetrate some distance upstream. However, fish of most species at Kakadu spend their entire lives in fresh water, for instance eel tailed catfish, grunters, gudgeons, gobies, hardy heads and perchlets. About 15 per cent of Kakadu fish species are diadromous, that is they breed in the saline estuaries or coastal waters and after breeding migrate to freshwater bodies in the Park. Here they put on weight feeding on the abundant food. Diadromous species of prime interest to commercial and recreational fishermen are silver barramundi or giant perch *Lates calcarifer* and ox eye herrings *Megalops cyprinoides*. Fork tailed catfish *Arius leptaspis*, eels and most mullet species undertake similar migrations.

A number of breeding strategies are employed by fish in Kakadu. These include live bearing (river whaler sharks and stingrays); mouth brooding (female saratogas carry their eggs in their mouths whereas it is a male responsibility for fork tailed catfish and cardinal fish *Glossamia aprion*); nest building and guarding (eel tailed catfish *Neosilurus* species, some grunters,

Tiger scat fish. (I.J.M.)

gobies and gudgeons); attaching eggs to submerged objects (rainbow fish *Melanotaenia nigrans* and long toms *Strongylura kreffti*); scattering demersal eggs over the substrate (hardy heads and spangled grunters *Leiopotherapon unicolor*); and laying pelagic eggs (archer fish, ox eye herrings and silver barramundi).

Two fish species are believed to be endemic to Kakadu, namely Arnhem Land blue eyes *Pseudomugil tenellus* and black anal finned grunters *Pingalla midgleyi*. Some freshwater fish have remarkable disjunct distributions in the Park. For example fork tailed catfish *Arius australis* and *A. proximus*, toothless eel tailed catfish *Anodontiglanis dahli* and primitive archer fish *Toxotes lorentzi* are found in the fresh waters of the South Alligator River but surprisingly not in the waters of the adjacent catchment of the East Alligator. Some fish species are confined to the clear waters near the escarpment. These include primitive archer fish recorded only from Irian Jaya and the South Alligator River, the rare Gilbert's grunters *Pingalla gilberti*, sharp nosed grunters *Syncomistes butleri* and saratogas *Scleropages jardini*.

Three fish species are of special interest, archer fish *Toxotes chatareus*, silver barramundi and saratogas.

Archer fish are carnivores which feed mainly on swimming or floating animals but also on flying insects. To capture their flying prey they spit droplets of water with uncanny accuracy for a distance of up to 1.5 metres. The jet of water is produced by a sudden compression of the gill covers to force water through a deep longitudinal groove along the roof of the mouth. The accuracy is remarkable for, since the eyes are under water, the fish have to correct for refraction at the water surface besides making an adjustment for curvature in the trajectory of the water jet. Presumably practice makes perfect.

Silver barramundi are featured in many X-ray style Aboriginal paintings. Angling stories abound about silver barramundi, which reputedly grow to over 1.5 metres in length and over 60 kilograms in weight. They provide excellent sport fishing and, being highly esteemed for the texture and taste of their flesh, are important commercially. They are rarely taken at sea distant from land but are usually caught in freshwater rivers and creeks, in billabongs and in coastal waters where there is some mixing of fresh water. Spawning and breeding occur in the coastal waters and mangrove swamps and, after spending the early part of their lives there, young fish migrate inland up the rivers, preferably

An archer fish. (G.L.M.)   Salmon catfish. (I.J.M.)

65

slow-moving rivers with a high silt load. They grow rapidly in the inland waters where there is abundant food. As the rivers and creeks dry up in the dry season, mature barramundi may be confined to land-locked billabongs and have to await the wet before they can travel downstream to breed. Barramundi change their sex with age; the smaller individuals are males. At Kakadu, sex inversion to females occurs when the fish are about 90 centimetres long at 6 or 7 years of age. Prolonged taking of large fish can upset the sex ratio and endanger the species by the loss of breeding females. There is concern that the population of silver barramundi in northern Australia is being seriously depleted by excessive fishing pressure.

Fossilised saratogas have been found in rocks 50 million years old. As descendants of an ancient line of fish, saratogas are considered one of the few fish species to have completed its entire evolution in fresh water. The eggs are hatched in the mouth of females and the fingerlings are guarded for several days after moving out. The females recall them to their mouths if danger threatens.

Whilst the fish stocks of the Park are generally healthy, natural fish kills have been observed at the onset of the wet season when the first increased stream flows enter previously isolated billabongs. This mortality may be caused by various factors and possibly results from a combination of the influx of natural fish poisons washed from trees and shrubs and relatively acid run-off water containing biotoxic levels of aluminium.

Insects Kakadu harbours a vast array of insect species. Insects such as cicadas can be very noisy at times. Entomologists estimate there are about 10 000 different kinds of insects at Kakadu. Already about half that number have been collected but not all have been described scientifically. In particular many different kinds of flies, moths, butterflies and beetles are present. Whilst little is known of the biology of insects in the Park, undoubtedly they play an important role in the ecology of the area as plant pollinators, decomposers of organic matter, and as food for other animals. Aboriginal people collect the honey of the native stingless bees from the hives built in trees.

A striking example of unusual insect behaviour occurs at Kakadu in the dry season when insects which normally live in open woodland migrate to relatively moist patches of monsoon rainforest. There they cluster together in aggregations containing hundreds or thousands of individuals at favoured sites on the trunks of trees such as the fig *Ficus virens* or on shaded vertical rock surfaces. Usually the aggregations consist of a single species. Insects recorded as behaving in this way include stink bugs *Coptosoma lyncea*, grass feeding bugs *Leptocorisa acuta*, pod sucking bugs *Gralliclava australiensis*, crow butterflies *Euploea core* and *E. sylvester*, blowflies *Euphumosia papua*, butterflies *Danaus affinis* and flies of the families Dolichopodidae and Milichiidae. If the aggregations are disturbed a burst of swirling flight is triggered off, sometimes accompanied by an audible buzzing, before the insects settle again, usually at the same place. This mass flight behaviour is thought to be a defence mechanism, the aggregations reinforcing the natural defences of individual insects and serving to confuse or alarm predators. Many insects which behave in this way have volatile, repugnant scents or harmful body fluids derived from toxic food plants.

Dragonfly. (I.J.M.)

Orange lacewing butterfly. (G.L.M.)

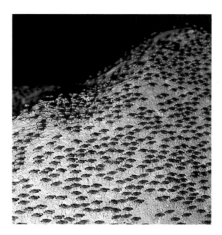

Flies congregated on a rock face. (I.J.M.)

Perhaps the most impressive insects of the Park are Leichhardt's grasshoppers *Petasida ephippigera*, some of the world's largest and most colourful grasshoppers. About 6 centimetres long, these vivid blue and orange grasshoppers were originally collected by the explorer Leichhardt but then not recorded again until rediscovered by biologists over a century later in the early 1970s. Since they feed on only certain kinds of aromatic shrubs, they are restricted to a few locations in the Park where they may be fairly abundant.

Other colourful insects are dragonflies; some seventy kinds have been recorded at Kakadu. As the floodwaters recede, large flocks of adult dragonflies appear, swooping or hovering over the water. Shallow temporary waters, billabongs, streams and rivers

Mayfly resting on mangrove flower. (I.J.M.)

A robber fly, a predator of other insects. (I.J.M.)

Stink bug sucks eucalypt and other plant saps. (C.T.)

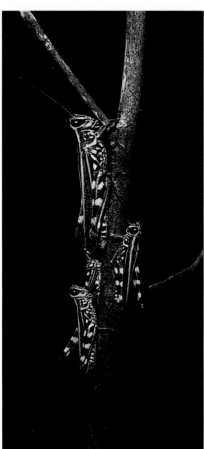

Grasshoppers. (I.J.M.)

each have their own characteristic dragonfly species. Dragonflies, both larvae and adults, are carnivores preying on smaller insects. In turn, they are preyed on by birds and fish. Two species of dragonflies found at Kakadu have only been recorded from streams draining the Arnhem Land escarpment. Since they have taxonomic affinities with the dragonflies of southern temperate Australia they may be relict populations of once widespread species or may be relatively recent newcomers to Kakadu.

Termites are common in the Park and, though a relatively primitive group of insects, have a complex social structure with specialised castes of large queens, tiny kings, workers and soldiers. The staple diet of termites is cellulose, which is broken down by intestinal protozoa and bacteria. In their search for cellulose termites can seriously damage park buildings and kill small trees. Giant termites *Mastotermes darwiniensis* are present in the Park and probably are Australia's most destructive insects. Found nowhere else than northern tropical Australia, they are sole survivors of a family of termites only known from other continents by fossils 200 million years old.

Termite mounds of various shapes and sizes constructed by different species can be seen. Some open woodland landscapes at Kakadu have many large columnar termite mounds, often over 3 metres tall. The mounds are built of clay by colonies of grass eating termites *Nasutitermes triodiae* and are believed to persist for over 100 years. The outer layer is very hard and internally there is a network of galleries and compartments in which the colony lives in an environment sheltered from climatic extremes. Some scientists believe that the deep grooves of the mound surface help to regulate the internal temperature. When buffaloes rub against a mound the base becomes smooth and narrower for up to 1.5 metres, creating a pedestal effect.

Other creatures may live in termite mounds, for example insects which feed on young termites or captive insects fed by termites which eat the insect secretions. Some kinds of parrots and kingfishers build their nests in termite mounds and monitor lizards may also lay their eggs in them. Termites have many natural enemies including frogs, reptiles and mammals. Echidnas *Tachyglossus aculeatus* have strong foreclaws which enable them to break into termite mounds and, by extending their long sticky tongues into the mound galleries, they are able to feast on termites.

Ants may be viewed as troublesome insects by people but they play an important role in the biology of the Park. Like termites they have a highly developed caste structure. Several ant species are present at Kakadu, and perhaps the most interesting is the relatively common green tree ant *Oecophylla smaragdina*. If disturbed, green tree ants become very aggressive, biting intruders and squirting formic acid on the wound, a painful experience for the recipient. They feed on the excretions of captive aphids and scale insects. Green tree ants are remarkable in that they act as a highly organised, close-knit community. The arboreal nest is built of tree leaves bound together with silk threads secreted by larvae brought from other nests by worker ants for this purpose. Worker ants form long lines along which

Shield bugs. (I.J.M.)

Green ants nest building. (C.T.)

69

leaves and other things are moved and, if necessary, cling to one another and toil with their jaws and legs to provide communal power. The ability of worker ants to move objects much larger and heavier than themselves considerable distances and up trees to the nests derives from their remarkable facility to combine their efforts in the common interest.

■

Spiders, molluscs and crustaceans   As yet, no detailed surveys and studies of invertebrates other than insects have been completed in the Park but they are known to be abundant in certain habitats. The presence of many spiders at Kakadu is evident early in the morning when the dew has settled on their webs.

Wolf spider eating an ant. (I.J.M.)

A field reconnaissance in the mangrove swamp forests revealed the presence of a variety of spiders, molluscs and crustaceans, some being very numerous in these localities. Many had not been recorded previously in tropical Australia. In all, twenty-six species of spiders were collected and some, such as a species of wolf spider, are believed to be new to science. Of the thirty-four different kinds of molluscs, mostly snails, found in the mangroves, five are new species not recorded previously. The list of seventy-five kinds of mangrove crustaceans, mainly crabs, includes eight new species.

A preliminary survey of the monsoon forests recorded almost 200 species of spiders of which about two-thirds are confined to the monsoon forest. Sedentary spiders, that is those which rely

Snails live in the humidity of the rainforest. (I.J.M.)

70

A mangrove crab. (I.J.M.)

Web building *Gasteracantha* spiders
have rectangular, multicoloured
abdomens. (M.P.)

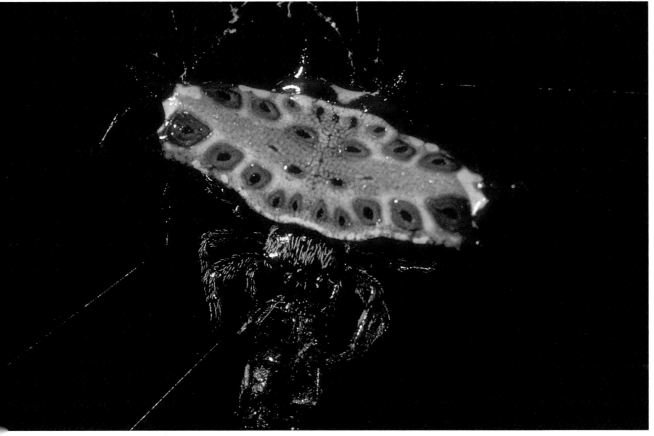

on webs to catch their prey, are in a minority in this forest type
and most spiders are free-ranging hunters.

Some Kakadu spiders are fascinating mimics. Hard bodied
spiders *Poecilothomisus speciosus* imitate dying insects on trees and
shrubs by quivering on their backs awaiting the arrival of much
larger huntsman spiders, which suddenly find they have become
the prey and not the hunters. Other mimics are crab spiders
Amyciaea bimaculata, which are green, distinctly waisted and with
two dark spots. At first glance they appear to be green ants and
this deception probably permits them to infiltrate the ranks of
green ants on which they feed.

Plants   Compared with other areas of similar size in northern Australia, the flora of Kakadu National Park is remarkably rich in species, some endemic. Although only preliminary surveys have been completed, almost 900 different kinds of plants have been recorded and undoubtedly more remain to be discovered. Botanists estimate the final figure will be about 1200 or nearly half of all Top End (north Australia) species. This floristic richness arises from the multiplicity of land and water habitats in the Park.

With such a profusion of plant species it is hard to decide which is most characteristic or symbolic of the Kakadu scene. Perhaps three species of pandanus best fulfil this role as a group for they occur in several major landscape types and give an

Stands of *Pandanus spiralis* on South Alligator River floodplain. (I.J.M.)

impression of tropical vegetation. The palm-like trees of *Pandanus spiralis* are a distinctive feature along the Arnhem Highway and the eastern side of the South Alligator floodplain, where they form extensive, rather open stands. Their reddish kernels or nuts are extremely nourishing and eaten by Aborigines. Trees of *P. basedowii* live on the dry sandstone escarpment and plateau where their large stilt roots provide stability. Trees of *P. aquaticus* occupy a very different niche for they grow along the edges of creeks and billabongs and at times are totally submerged in the wet season.

This diversity of plants at Kakadu, differing in size, form and ecological aptitude, represents a botanical storehouse of inestimable utility to people. Already, about 150 species have been found to be of horticultural value as outdoor or indoor

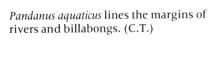
Pandanus aquaticus lines the margins of rivers and billabongs. (C.T.)

Pandanus basedowii survives on the sandstone escarpment; its stilt roots penetrate deeply between rocks. (C.T.)

plants. The potential of the Kakadu flora as a source of genetic material for horticultural and breeding purposes remains largely unexplored. This is a powerful argument for its protection.

■

Floral display The plants of Kakadu rival the animals in their individual beauty and variety of shapes and life cycles. Although not having the spectacularly vivid wildflower display of Western Australia, Kakadu is a rewarding place for anyone interested in wildflowers and in botany generally. Throughout the year one species after another comes into flower or fruit. Various nectar-feeding birds and insects and fruit-eating mammals such as flying foxes synchronise their movements and breeding patterns with the flowering and fruiting sequence.

Darwin woollybutt flowers. (I.J.M.)

Several brightly coloured flowering species give their best colour display in the dry season when, as it happens, more people are in the Park. Certain kinds of trees shed their leaves in the dry to reduce water loss and this provides a good opportunity to see their flowers. Typical of these dry season deciduous trees are kapoks *Cochlospermum fraseri*, cottonwoods *Bombax ceiba* and kurrajongs *Brachychiton paradoxum*. Good specimens of kapok trees occur near the Park Headquarters and along the roadsides of woodland areas. The trees carry bright yellow flowers and the light, fluffy kapok surrounding the seeds looks like cotton wool. Cottonwoods, widely distributed in riverine and monsoon forests, are very large trees with thorny trunks. Good specimens can be seen at the East Alligator Crossing and near the bridge

Flowers of *Eucalyptus phoenicea*. (C.

Kurrajong flowers. (C.T.)

over the South Alligator River. The flowers are large, red and waxy and the seeds are covered with kapok, which was used by Aboriginal people for body decoration. Trunks of cottonwood trees were used by Aborigines to make dugout canoes. Kurrajong trees occur throughout the woodland areas; one is in front of the Blue Paintings Art Site at Nourlangie. The small trumpet-like flowers are bright red, the fruit is edible and string for Aboriginal collecting bags is made from the bark.

Other tree species retain their leaves in the dry but still make a significant contribution to the floral display. Eucalypts such as Darwin woollybutts *Eucalyptus miniata* on the deeper woodland soils and *E. phoenicea* on the boulder-strewn escarpment slopes have vivid blossoms ranging in colour from orange to yellow.

Kapok tree flowers. (C.T.)

Cottonwood tree flower. (I.J.M.)

75

The white trunks of eucalypts are attractive. (C.T.)

Grevillea pteridifolia flowers. (C.T.)

76

Other eucalypts, for instance ghost gums *E. papuana*, common along the margins of the floodplains, produce in the early wet season clusters of cream blossom attractive to lorikeets and flying foxes. White gums *E. alba* and ghost gums add to the beauty of the landscape because of their strikingly white to grey trunks. Specimen trees can be seen at Nourlangie Rock and Muirella Park. Gardenias *Gardenia megasperma* are common in the north of the Park and abundant alongside the walking trail at Ubirr (Obiri Rock). They have gnarled and twisted trunks and bear white, sweetly scented flowers. The many species of *Melaleuca*, *Acacia* and *Cassia* produce a mass of colour in season. Grevilleas vary in size from trees to semi-prostrate shrubs and as a group have particularly showy and unusual flowers. There are about

Prostrate *Grevillea* flowers. (I.J.M.)

ten different kinds in the Park, some unnamed and possibly endemic. Trees of *Grevillea pteridifolia* grow to about 10 metres tall in open forest and eucalypt woodland. Good specimens are noticeable along the roadsides of damper areas. The vivid orange bottlebrush flowers set against a background of spindly silver green foliage are very attractive. Many shrubs in the Park bear showy flowers. Plants of *Hibiscus symonii*, common around the sandstone outliers, have large pink blossoms. Turkey bushes *Calytrix exstipulata* form thickets up to 3 metres tall in wooded areas and produce masses of brilliantly coloured mauve flowers.

The herbs and grasses are not outdone by woody plants in the beauty of their floral displays, especially those growing on the floodplains and billabongs. Some billabong margins become a

Grevillea heliosperma flowers. (C.T.)

Fern fronds provide an attractive feature to the forest floor. (C.T.)

Ipomea on coastal sand beaches. (I.J.M.)

The water lily *Nymphoides hydrocharoides* forms a yellow carpet along billabong margins. (C.T.)

Delicate spinifex flowerheads. (I.J.M.)

The stinkhorn fungus emits a strong smell to attract insects, which aid spore dispersal. (I.J.M.)

carpet of colour when species such as *Nymphoides hydrocharoides* bloom to produce a mass of bright yellow. In swampy areas lotus lilies *Nelumbo nucifera* carry huge red flowers and water lilies *Nymphaea gigantea* produce flowers grading in colour from white to blue set against a background of round floating leaves. The flowering heads of grasses, though lacking in bright colour, provide an attractive feature when illuminated by the sun's rays. Non-flowering plants such as ferns, mosses and fungi add colour and interest to the forest shade.

Flowers of the water lily *Nymphaea gigantea* vary from white to purple. (C.T.)

Red lotus lilies are making a comeback as the number of buffaloes decreases. (C.T.)

Hibiscus flower. (I.J.M.)

Turkey bushes produce masses of flowers. (C.T.)

The insectivorous *Drosera petiolaris* captures insects on its sticky leaves. (C.T.)

Interior of Rhizophora mangrove forest showing stilt roots. (I.J.M.)

Aerial roots (pneumatophores) in mangrove swamp. (I.J.M.)

Plant communities   The vegetation is a mosaic of distinctive plant assemblages, or communities, which developed over the ages in response to changing ecological conditions. Depending on site conditions, they differ greatly in structure and in the combination of plant species present. The low, dispersed spinifex vegetation of the sandstone plateau, for instance, is very dissimilar to the tall, continuous, highly structured monsoon rainforest. The broad spatial distribution of plant communities is shown in Fig. 4.

Forests and more open woodlands of numerous kinds cover over half of the Park area. The coastal mangrove forests, with a maximum height of about 20 metres, contain over twenty species of mangrove trees. Various algae, lichens and fungi are associated with the mangroves. The most common trees are *Avicennia marina*, *Rhizophora stylosa*, *Ceriops tagal* and *Lumnitzera racemosa*. The mangrove trees are arranged in distinct species zones according to the topographic position within the intertidal area. The seaward zones are dominated by species more tolerant of salt, such as *R. stylosa* and *Sonneratia alba*, whilst *C. tagal* and *L. racemosa* border the inland mangrove edge where inundation by sea water is infrequent and salinity less. Some mangrove stands are very dense and in places about fifty stems of *C. tagal* have been recorded per square metre.

Life is not easy for the plants of the mangrove swamps because the forest floor is submerged under sea water at high tide. Various means are adopted by mangrove trees to overcome the salinity problem. The roots of some mangroves are able physiologically to reduce salt intake whilst other mangroves get rid of surplus salt by excreting it from their leaves. Because of the

Escarpment rainforest community in plateau valley. (C.T.)

Mangrove forest community bordering tidal section of East Alligator River. (C.T.)

tidal flooding and waterlogging of the soil, oxygen uptake by the mangrove roots is difficult. This has been solved by having specialised stilt or prop roots which arch outwards from the tree trunks above water level. Other short, spike-like roots called pneumatophores stick up from the ground and have a spongy interior in which sufficient oxygen is stored when the roots are exposed at low tide to enable them to survive the tidal flooding.

The Kakadu monsoon rainforest communities are restricted to areas with permanent underground or surface fresh water in the sandstone gorges and along the margins of floodplains, rivers, fresh water streams and pools. They resemble the rainforests of South-East Asia in having a relatively continuous evergreen tree canopy, trees with buttress roots and, in places, a highly

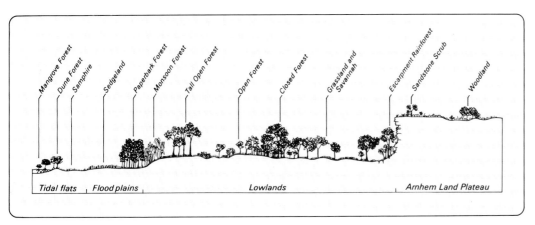

Fig. 4 Vegetation cross section

81

developed community structure of trees, vines, epiphytic mosses, lichens, ferns and orchids. However, they contain fewer plant species than Asian rainforests because of their limited area and because they consist of small, isolated patches, sometimes highly disturbed by buffaloes and pigs. The rainforest patches are of considerable scientific interest, being relicts of the vegetation of a past climatic era. Since they are moist and relatively fire free, they have long served as key refuges for many different kinds of plants and animals. Two main kinds of rainforest have been recognised, escarpment rainforest and rainforests bordering the coastline and floodplains.

The major tree species of the sandstone escarpment rainforest is *Allosyncarpia ternata*, which often occurs as uniform blocks.

Coastal rainforest community with emergent palms. (C.T.)

Individuals grow up to 35 metres tall. Surprisingly, this species of large and distinctive evergreen trees was not described by botanists until 1976. Since the large seeds are not taken by birds and other animals, dispersal is poor and the ground immediately below the tree crowns may be covered with germinating seedlings. The ferns *Drynaria quercifolia* and *Cheilanthes fragillima* are common in the sandstone rainforest.

The rainforest bordering the floodplains and coastline has a more variable tree cover with the evergreen trees *Ganophyllum falcatum* and milkwoods *Alstonia actinophylla* being common. Figs, cluster figs *Ficus racemosa* and banyan figs *F. virens*, poisonous itchy trees *Barringtonia acutangula* and cottonwoods *Bombax ceiba* also occur, as well as climbing plants such as *Abrus precatorius* and

Buttress roots of rainforest trees. (C.T.)

East Alligator River rainforest community. (C.T.)

Aerial roots of banyan fig in rainforest. (C.T.)

Dominant tree of escarpment rainforest *Allosyncarpia ternata*. (C.T.)

Open eucalypt woodland. (C.T.)

Gymnanthera nitida. The palms *Carpentaria acuminata* and *Livistona benthamii* are present in both sandstone and lowland monsoon rainforest. The cheeky yam *Amorphophallus variabilis*, which has a heavy, underground, edible tuber, is a rainforest species with an unusual pollination mechanism. The large red flowers only last for a few days, during which they give off a powerful stench of rotting meat to attract blowflies and beetles, which serve as pollinators.

On the floodplains there are extensive paperbark swamp forests. Here the water-table is high throughout the year and the ground may be flooded during the wet. Nevertheless, these forests are sometimes subjected to damaging fires in the dry season. The paper-like bark of the dominant *Melaleuca* trees

Paperbark swamp community in the wet season. (C.T.)

enables fire to extend high into the canopy and, once ignited, the peaty soil and thick litter may burn and smoulder for a long time in the dry season. The two most abundant species of large paperbarks are the broad-leaved tea trees *Melaleuca leucadendron* and *M. argentea* which grow up to 20 metres tall. Some associated species are largely confined to these swamps; epiphytic orchids *Cymbidium canaliculatum*, for instance, grow almost exclusively on paperbarks. The raised banks of the billabongs and streams of the floodplains may be lined with small clumps of screw palm *Pandanus spiralis* trees.

The drier woodlands are dominated by eucalypts, up to 25 metres tall. With increasing aridity the dry forests of the lowland hills grade into open woodland, savannah and eventually grassland vegetation. Some twenty-eight eucalypt species have

Billabong lily community. (C.T.)

Eleocharis swamp community on floodplains. (C.T.)

The floating aquatic fern *Azolla* may cover the water surface. (C.T.)

been recorded at Kakadu; apparently three have not been described previously. The two most common eucalypts are woollybutts *Eucalyptus miniata* and stringybarks *E. tetrodonta*. These occur as single species stands or mixed together in varying proportions. Other tree species associated with dry woodland are bloodwoods *E. bleeseri* and *E. polycarpa*, ghost gums *E. papuana*, ironwoods *Erythrophleum chlorostachys* and the sand palms *Livistona humilis* and *L. inermis*. Small trees and shrubs of numerous species of *Acacia*, *Grevillea* and *Terminalia* form a broken shrub layer under the tree canopy. The ground vegetation of grasses and herbs is sparse in the more closed forests but in open woodlands and grasslands can be very dense and occasionally over 1.5 metres tall when native *Sorghum* grasses are present.

Except where there are stretches of open water, a dense mat of grasses and sedges covers the vast, flat floodplains of the northern section of the Park. The impeded drainage causes widespread waterlogging of the soil and the consequent development of swamps of *Eleocharis* and *Oryza* species and sedgeland of *Fimbristylis* species. The spiky foliage of the spiked rush *Eleocharis dulcis* is used as nesting material by magpie geese, which also feed on its tuberous corms. Seed of the spiked rush and wild rice *Oryza meridionalis* are good feed for geese and the aquatic grasses *Chrysopogon latifolius* and *Phragmites karka* provide shelter and nesting places for many different kinds of birds. The billabongs have an attractive flora dominated by water lilies of various species. The floating aquatic fern *Azolla pinnata* may multiply rapidly and become abundant to cover the water surface.

In the harsher environments of the Park, the vegetation gives a very incomplete cover. Thus the tidal mud flats have an open samphire *Arthrocnemum* community of salt-tolerant shrubs, herbaceous plants, sedges and grasses. Large areas of the escarpment and plateau are bare sandstone but, where there are pockets of soil, a varied heathlike community persists of leguminous and myrtaceous shrubs accompanied by small herbaceous plants and grasses. The spinifex grasses, species of *Eriachne*, *Plectrachne* and *Triodia*, form individual hummocks and in more favourable places dense mats.

Aboriginal use of plants   Plants have long played an important role in the life of Aboriginal people at Kakadu. Not only do Aborigines have specific names for several hundred plant species but they also possess a remarkably detailed knowledge of their morphology, biology, ecology and usefulness. Here it is only possible to give a brief account of a few uses made of some plants.

Plants provide Aboriginal people with a nutritious and varied diet. Many kinds of shoots, fruits, seeds, nuts, roots and underground stems are eaten. Bush plums *Terminalia ferdinandiana* have small, edible fruits which contain a remarkably high concentration of vitamin C. Other sought-after fruits include red apples *Syzygium suborbiculare*, white apples *S. bleeseri*, species of figs *Ficus* and green plums *Buchanania obovata*. Green plums are picked when ripe in the early wet season and coated in a slurry of red ochre before being stored in caches in the sandstone for consumption in the following wet season months when fruit is scarce. The tender apical shoots of *Livistona* palms are eaten raw or lightly roasted and the large seeds of red lotus lilies *Nelumbo nucifera* have a tasty nutty flavour. Tubers of many yam species (for example species of *Dioscorea*) are rich in carbohydrates and may be eaten raw or, depending on the species, carefully soaked and crushed to remove any toxins present.

Some plants are used to flavour the meat of native animals. The herb *Corynotheca lateriflora* is reputed to make the flesh of emus and kangaroos more tasty and the leaves of various *Melaleuca* species are valued as good flavourings for the meat of goannas, rock possums, crocodiles and fish. Sheets of bark from paperbark trees are used to cover various animal foods for cooking in underground ovens; the waterproof properties of the bark help to hold in moisture and steam the meat. In times of drought, drinkable water can be obtained by tapping galls on the trunks of paperbark trees.

Aboriginal people also recognise that specific plants nourish certain insects, birds, fish, turtles and mammals eaten by them. They identify at least six species of native bees and appreciate that the quality and flavour of the honey depends on the plant species worked by the bees. Plants are also used as a fishing aid. The fruits of certain species are thrown into the water to attract fish to the banks of waterholes where they can be speared. The bark and leaves of *Owenia vernicosa* and species of *Cassia*, *Barringtonia* and *Tephrosia* are used as poisons to stun fish, which can then be collected when they float to the surface.

Harvest of nutritious white apples, green plums and black plums. (P.W.)

Open samphire community of tidal flats. (C.T.)

Making a didjeridoo requires skill and a knowledge of wood. (P.W.)

Aboriginal grinding stone and hollow for pulverising seeds and fruit. (P.W.)

Plants also provide for other material needs of Aborigines. Trees and shrubs supply firewood for cooking and the inherent burning characteristics of different woods are recognised, some burning slowly whilst others give a quick heat. Dugout canoes, spears, fire sticks, music sticks, fighting sticks, digging sticks and didjeridoos are made from the wood of trees or shrubs selected for their particular properties. Tree bark, particularly *Melaleuca* and *Eucalyptus* bark, is the traditional material for roofing field shelters and for making rafts and containers for food or water, and provides string for weaving carrier bags. The bark of paperbarks is used for wrapping up human corpses for burial. Stems of the sedge *Cyperus decompositus* are used to make traditional fish traps and nets and the stem fibres when exposed by chewing serve as paint brushes for rock artwork. Bark paintings are done on the bark of stringybarks *Eucalyptus tetrodonta* using various plant gums as pigment binders. The juice of some orchids is a traditional binder and fixative for the pigments used in painting. Wood of evergreen milkwood trees *Alstonia actinophylla* is used for wood carvings and the rough leaves of figs *Ficus scobina* serve as sandpaper to smooth wooden objects, particularly spears. The seed cones of the only *Banksia* native to the Northern Territory, *Banksia dentata*, make good hair combs. Mats and baskets plaited from the leaves of *Pandanus spiralis* and rushes are coloured with various plant dyes, for instance those obtained from the subterranean bark of *Coelospermum reticulatum* and the bulbs of the bloodroots *Haemodorum* species. Plants also provide decorative objects such as arm bands, fibres woven for clothing, children's rattles and spinning tops. Leaves of immature swamp bloodwoods *Eucalyptus polycarpa* are inflated to make balloon toys.

Many kinds of plants are used in various ways for medicinal purposes. The smoke of some plants, such as yams *Dioscorea sativa*, is believed to have healing or purification properties and other smoke is regarded as having a cleansing effect, for instance during childbirth. The fumes from crushed leaves of certain plants are inhaled as cures for different maladies. Medicinal plant solutions are made to be drunk or applied externally, for instance to cure headache, earache, toothache, chest pains, sore eyes and diarrhoea. A solution from mistletoes *Decaisnina brittenii* is used to treat open sores and wounds. Where the effective chemical compounds are difficult to extract, the preparation of the medicinal solution may involve complex procedures with repeated crushing and soaking of the plant material. Some kinds of plants are used as repellants, the sap of paperbark orchids *Cymbidium canaliculatum* being rubbed on the legs to keep leeches at bay. Smoke generated by burning certain plants is used to repel mosquitoes.

Having evolved in diverse ways since life began, the native plants contain a vast array of chemical substances and undoubtedly many of these have application for medicinal and other purposes. Traditional Aboriginal use and knowledge of the properties of native plants can provide guidance as to the potential use of plant substances in contemporary society if only we are wise enough to take the opportunity to benefit from this experience.

A HERITAGE FOR THE FUTURE

National park concept The national park movement in Australia began in earnest with the establishment of the Royal National Park near Sydney over a century ago in 1879. Since then the number of national parks and other protected nature conservation areas has grown until they now account for over 4 per cent of the surface of the continent. To those who enjoy nature and believe wildlife should be protected in natural surroundings, national parks are an essential part of contemporary living.

Why this major change in rural land use occurred at a time of increasing urbanisation and industrialisation is unclear. Perhaps it is an expression of growing public awareness of the special spiritual and material values which wilderness and wildlife provide for people and of the personal commitment of dedicated individuals to conserve examples of natural areas. Pressure to set aside land for nature conservation purposes is reinforced where it is associated with the protection of a unique cultural heritage as at Kakadu National Park.

The modern concept of national parks recognises they are for the benefit of people and, whilst they can cater for different uses (e.g. recreation, education and nature conservation), these uses must be compatible with husbanding and appreciating the natural and cultural resources. Kakadu National Park contains a diversity of natural systems (ecosystems) which vary in their capacity to provide for different uses.

■

Management If national parks are not to deteriorate through uncontrolled use, they have to be managed. Since there is an infinity of management options in relation to the intensity and kinds of management, it is necessary to clarify management objectives. In this way the most effective management system can be determined and implemented to achieve these objectives.

Unfortunately, most people going to national parks are unaware of the many facets to park management and tend to see things from their own, limited, personal perspectives. Divergent

Traditional Aboriginal fishing. (M.P.)

A care for wildlife. (I.J.M.)

Aboriginal trainees take an interest in archaeological investigations. (I.J.M.)

public views often emerge on the use to be made of particular places in national parks or about specific park policies. In these circumstances it is important to ensure people are fully informed and an acceptable resolution of the different views is achieved, bearing in mind the long-term consequences of any decisions taken. Usually with informed discussion most issues can be resolved satisfactorily but on occasion some user groups may feel disappointed when, in the interests of the community as a whole, it proves impossible to meet their wishes fully.

Exemplary park management can only be obtained through experience and detailed knowledge of a park's resources as the basis for the implementation of sound planning in sympathy with public opinion. Comprehensive surveys of the cultural and natural resources of Kakadu National Park are being completed by the Park staff, various research agencies and individual experts. Public involvement in planning is attempted primarily through the process leading to the production of a management plan as required under the Commonwealth *National Parks and Wildlife Conservation Act 1975*. This involves obtaining at an early stage public participation and views on what is needed through newspaper advèrtisements. A draft management plan is then prepared which takes account of these views. Public comment is sought on the draft plan and finally ministerial and parliamentary approval is obtained for a revised final version of the plan. This procedure is strengthened by seeking the advice of local groups having special interests and expertise in various aspects of park management.

The preparation of a management plan is a task calling for great skill in the assessment and integration of diverse ideas and facts in order to arrive at a practical working arrangement having public support. A management plan provides background information on the ecology and administration of a park, identifies the aims of management and prescribes how these aims will be achieved over the period of the plan. The first plan of management for Kakadu, covering a period of nearly five years, came into force on 2 April 1981. In the long term, park management is based on a sequence of management plans each building on the previous ones.

National parks, like city parks, museums and art galleries, are expensive to establish and run properly and their management places demands on the public purse both for capital and operating costs. Kakadu is no exception and being so remote costs are high and development is largely constrained by government budgetary allocations. Furthermore, the wet season places restrictions on management and the types of facilities that can be provided. For example, the high water-tables and flooding pose special difficulties for the design of ablution, lavatory, road and other facilities.

A vital ingredient of good management is the dedication of the staff. Rangers and ancillary staff are responsible for the day to day running of the Park. Support specialists advise on particular subjects such as Aboriginal art, wildlife, tourism, fire, interpretation, staff training, engineering and architecture. Living in a remote tropical environment of great biological and cultural interest has its rewards but there are disadvantages, particularly for staff with children. For staff morale it is important to have reasonable accommodation available. Staff houses specially designed for living in extreme tropical conditions have been built. The isolation and remoteness also create a need to assist the staff to keep up to date with park developments elsewhere.

As part of a determined policy to develop Aboriginal management skills, and so enable them to take an ever greater role in management, special training courses have been held for interested Aborigines. Aboriginal trainees are selected by the Aboriginal people to undertake training courses in park management lasting for one year or longer. The successful male and female students are available for employment as park rangers. It has become clear that Aboriginal people have much to contribute through their remarkable ecological understanding of the interrelationships between living things and environmental conditions. Senior Aborigines, appointed to the Park staff as cultural advisers, have been particularly helpful in contributing their experience and wisdom in the running of the Park. The combination of Aboriginal and European knowledge being applied in managing Kakadu adds a new and rewarding dimension to the scope of park management. Aboriginal people elsewhere in Australia are now looking towards the Kakadu example for possible application on traditional lands and there is considerable international interest in this co-operative approach.

■

Art sites Most people coming to Kakadu National Park wish to view Aboriginal rock art and to learn about the paintings. With the agreement of the Aboriginal people the spectacular rock art galleries at Ubirr (Obiri) and Burrunguy (Nourlangie Rock) have been selected as two centres to be developed for this purpose.

The interpretation of the rock art and the associated introduction of tourist facilities take many forms. So far as possible, park rangers are present to help visitors and conduct tours around the art galleries at the two main outdoor exhibition centres. Road access to both areas has been upgraded and facilities such as signposted walking tracks, litter bins, bench seats, shelters, site maps and interpretation notice boards are being provided progressively. Considerable attention is devoted to locating and designing any structures or site works to ensure they do not impose a jarring, artificial intrusion into the landscape setting. To avoid the noise of coaches and cars coming

Rock overhangs are important Aboriginal sites. (C.T.)

Rifle training by the Army for feral animal control. (I.J.M.)

91

Making a photographic record of rock paintings. (D.A.G.)

Installing silicon drip lines to protect rock paintings against water damage. (I.J.M.)

Protective fences at Aboriginal art sites serve as camera stands. (C.T.)

and going, vehicle parking places are located a comfortable walking distance from the art sites. The tracks from the parking areas to the rock art wind between tree clumps to create a feeling of unhurried detachment. Special arrangements are necessary for the elderly and infirm who find walking difficult. In the vicinity of the galleries, local rocks have been used as random paving to aid access to the galleries and as stepping stones for clambering up small rock faces to the shelters. Raised wooden walkways have been installed where appropriate at wetter areas. The stone paving and wooden walkways, by preventing soil disturbance in shelters and under overhangs, help to preserve important archaeological material and minimise dust being raised and deposited on the paintings as a result of people walking nearby.

The increasing number of people going to art sites poses a threat of vandalism. To prevent this, rangers patrol the more popular art sites, particularly during the dry season when more visitors are present. Because of the large number of art sites and the relatively small number of rangers, complete protection at all times is impossible. Fortunately, vandalism has not proved a major problem, apparently because people who have travelled far to see the Park tend to treat it with respect.

Often unthinkingly, people touch the rock paintings and in time this leads to deterioration. The Aboriginal people have long recognised the deleterious effects of people touching the paintings. A senior Aboriginal recalls: 'When I was a little boy if I touched those paintings my father might belt me with a stick, give me a hiding. We have to look after these paintings, keep

Wasp nest built over hand stencil. (I.J.M.)

them good for our kids coming up.' Such drastic measures are not available to the Park Service but the co-operation of the public in protecting art sites is being sought by making people aware of the importance of the art and the dangers it faces. The new viewing facilities, with discreet wooden barriers, allow improved access to sites and keep people at arm's length from the paintings but not so far as to make photography of the artwork unrewarding.

The rock paintings are also threatened by several natural processes. Inevitably paintings are lost or damaged by rock falls, but water is considered the most immediate serious damaging agent. Pigments are washed off paintings by water flowing across the art work or seeping from the rock. In addition,

Aboriginal rangers explain rock paintings. (C.T.)

subsurface water evaporates from the rock surface leaving salts and other minerals to cause exfoliation of painted surfaces.

Insects are another source of damage. Some wasps build mud nests on the paintings and termites may construct their mud galleries across some artwork. The major builders of mud nests at Kakadu are wasps *Sceliphron laetum*. These are readily identifiable, being predominantly black and yellow in colour, about 3 centimetres long with extended, narrow waists, and in flight their long legs hang conspicuously from their bodies. Females collect the mud and build the nests, each consisting of a series of cells. Before laying an egg in each cell and sealing the entrance, the female wasp stocks it with spiders on which the growing wasp larva feeds. Preliminary studies indicate that wasp nests are more frequent on relatively dry rock surfaces shaded from direct sunlight.

Mushroom-shaped termite mound caused by buffalo rubbing. (I.J.M.)

Damage may also be done to the rock art by plants. In certain situations lichens and plant roots grow over paintings. Another problem is that vegetation, particularly the branches and leaves of trees growing nearby, may rub against and obliterate the paintings when blown by the wind. Buffaloes rubbing against paintings have the same effect but this is less serious now because of the reduction in buffalo numbers.

Corrective measures taken to prevent these different kinds of damage include changing the water drainage pattern so as to direct water from caves and overhangs, installing silicon drip lines to divert surface water from the paintings, carefully removing wasp nests and termite galleries by hand, fencing sites against buffaloes and cutting back the vegetation at cave entrances or along the margins of rock overhangs. So far as possible, Aboriginal people are encouraged to participate in this protective work, in which they have shown great interest.

Feral animals Feral animals are considered here to be non-native animals gone wild. Dingoes are not regarded as feral animals because of their presence at Kakadu for thousands of years. The main feral animals causing damage at Kakadu are the more recent newcomers — buffaloes *Bubalus bubalis*, pigs *Sus scrofa*, cattle *Bos taurus*, horses *Equus caballus* (brumbies), cats *Felis catus* and to a lesser extent dogs *Canis familiaris*.

Of all feral animals, buffaloes have been the greatest management problem. The shipment of water buffaloes from Timor to Fort Wellington in 1828 was the forerunner of other shipments to various settlements in the Northern Territory over the following twenty years. The rationale for importation was to provide a source of fresh meat and draught animals for the settlements. When the settlements failed, the abandoned buffaloes spread widely and multiplied in the tropical environment of northern Australia where predators were few and there was food in plenty. Estimates suggest that, despite extensive shooting, the number of buffaloes in the Northern Territory had increased to about 200 000 by the 1960s. The major herds were concentrated on the coastal plains between the Adelaide and East Alligator Rivers. Twenty years later the estimate had increased by another 50 000.

A buffalo harvesting industry developed in the 1880s, and by the 1890s Paddy Cahill, a renowned buffalo hunter of great

Buffalo wallows.
(I.J.M.)

94

character based at Oenpelli, introduced shooting from horseback. The buffalo industry became a major employer of Aborigines and Aboriginal shooters such as Butcher Knight, Yorky Billy Alderson and Toby Gangale developed reputations as crack shots. The work was hard and dangerous. Aboriginal women washed and salted the hides in the buffalo hunters' camps. Payment was usually in kind and major attractions of the buffalo camps for Aboriginal people were sticks of trade tobacco called nicki nicki, other European stimulants, especially tea, clothing and useful items such as billy cans. Up to the late 1950s, buffaloes were shot principally for their hides and horns but later the meat was used for human and pet consumption. More recently live buffaloes have been exported to Asia.

Asian water buffaloes are featured in the tourist literature and on the logos of northern institutions. To many they are symbolic of the Top End, creating visions of the remote outback and of safari hunting as practised in Africa. They have been part of the romance of the northern wilderness scene for over a century. Whilst regarded as gentle domesticated animals in Asia, buffaloes in Australia are seen as large, wild animals with massive, spreading horns and a deserved reputation for ferocity. Undoubtedly they can be dangerous and will attack people.

Whilst opinions differ on the extent of environmental impact of buffaloes, it is now generally accepted that, by their grazing, trampling, wallowing and tree rubbing, these heavy, lumbering animals cause substantial environmental changes, often adversely affecting the natural vegetation, soil, waters, drainage and animal habitats. The channelling and gullying of entrenched buffalo trails are thought to contribute to the breaching of the natural levees of the tidal rivers and creeks, resulting in greater intrusion of salt water at high tides and the killing of paperbark swamps. In the mangrove and paperbark swamps and monsoon rainforests, buffaloes kill trees by rubbing and destroy sapling regrowth. In this way they open up the tree canopy, letting in sunlight and so promoting drying out and exposure to fire. Although buffaloes tend to remain within their particular territories, in the wet season there is a general movement to the drier upland country, where further vegetation damage is done and soil erosion often results. Buffaloes are also thought to have been responsible, at least in part, for the spread of weeds into the Park by carrying seeds in their hair and creating patches of bare

Vegetation is more luxuriant inside buffalo exclusion fence. (I.J.M.)

Historical photograph: a wounded buffalo bull in the grass. (Australia Archives)

95

Historical photograph: a buffalo bull turning on the shooters. (Australian Archives)

Buffalo wallows and tracks on floodplains. (C.T.)

soil which weeds readily colonise. Weeds may grow profusely around a buffalo carcass, apparently originating from viable seed in the gut of the dead animal.

General recognition of the adverse environmental impact of buffaloes is reinforced by observations at Kakadu. The population of buffaloes in Stage 1 of Kakadu National Park is believed to have been at least 20 000 at the time of proclamation but had been reduced to about a quarter of that by 1984. This reduction was followed by a marked increase in the abundance and distribution of certain native plants, some important to Aboriginals, for example the red lotus lily *Nelumbo nucifera*. Large areas of the Alligator Rivers floodplains, previously bare of vegetation at the end of the dry season, now have a continuous cover of grasses, sedges and herbs which is believed to have triggered off recolonisation by magpie geese and other birds. Similarly, buffalo exclusion plots installed by the CSIRO Division of Wildlife Research at Kapalga in Kakadu Stage 2 have shown a marked recovery of the perennial ground cover with the surface soil more friable and less compacted. These observations, together with decreased soil erosion as evidenced by reduced water turbidity, provide good reasons to control, if not eliminate, the exotic wild buffaloes from the Park.

Under the Brucellosis and Tuberculosis Eradication Campaign agreed on by Commonwealth, State and Territory Governments, there is additional pressure from agricultural interests to exterminate wild buffaloes in Australia. Diseased buffaloes threaten Australian beef sales, worth more than 3000 million dollars per annum, and it is planned Australia will have by 1992 a clean bill of health in relation to bovine tuberculosis and brucellosis. In addition, buffaloes and other feral animals could make more difficult the control of other exotic diseases which may spread to Australia. Possibly some disease-free domestic herds under strict veterinary control may be retained for their meat and as a reminder of the past.

Where buffaloes are abundant in the Park they are harvested by commercial contractors. When the numbers are so low that commercial utilisation is no longer economic, expert marksmen of the Park staff kill the buffaloes humanely using high-powered rifles. Sometimes helicopters are used to reach the more remote and inaccessible parts of the Park to carry out this work.

Wild pigs are found in most places in the Park where there is year-round access to water. Locally pigs cause environmental deterioration somewhat similar to that created by buffaloes for, like buffaloes but unlike native animals, they wallow and root in marshes, swamps and billabongs. Pigs, through their destruction of vegetation, change the habitat to the detriment of native animals. They also eat native frogs, snakes, small mammals and the eggs and nestlings of ground-dwelling birds, they muddy and foul the waters and are disease carriers. In their turn young pigs are eaten by dingoes. One danger is that the population of wild pigs might increase with the decline in buffalo numbers. Pigs are shot by the Park staff when the opportunity arises but, for economic reasons, the control effort as yet is not so intense as for buffaloes.

The few cattle and horses present are not thought to pose an immediate major hazard but some control may be required. Feral cats, usually seen near houses and along river and creek banks, are ruthless predators particularly of native birds and small mammals, and have to be eradicated. As in other national parks, dog control poses special management problems because Aborigines, residents of Jabiru and Park staff who live in the Park want to own dogs for various reasons. Furthermore, temporary visitors often arrive with their dogs after travelling long distances to see Kakadu and object strongly to any restrictions on the entry of their dogs. Unfortunately, dogs are sometimes abandoned by their owners or become lost in the Park. Some suffer terribly and die slowly of disease or starvation whilst others go wild and are very destructive of native wildlife. Dogs allowed to run wild may also be a nuisance to park visitors and residents.

Somewhat unusual feral animals are Asian house geckoes *Hemidactylus frenatus*. They are largely restricted to human settlements and apparently do not affect the native fauna except for native house geckoes *Gehyra australis*, which seem fewer in number where the introduced species occurs.

Weeds Weeds are opportunistic plant intruders not native to an area. Generally they are unable to become established where the native vegetation cover remains intact. At Kakadu weeds tend to occur at disturbed sites near settlements, along roadsides and at sites heavily infested with buffaloes and pigs. Jabiru is a potential source of alien plant species and the Australian National Parks and Wildlife Service has encouraged the town authority to use local species for landscaping purposes.

About seventy alien plant species have been reported growing in the Park including such potential weeds as the custard apple *Annona diversifolia*, cassia *Cassia elata*, Townsville stylo *Stylosanthes humilis*, para grass *Brachiaria mutica*, *Hyptis suaveolens* and the grass *Pennisetum pedicullatum*. Currently, two species of weeds, one terrestrial and the other aquatic, are of particular concern.

Giant sensitive plants *Mimosa pigra*, the leaves of which close up when touched, are widespread on neighbouring properties. If left alone *Mimosa* flowers profusely to produce a large amount of seed which remains viable for many years. Within a very few years, the native vegetation is replaced by dense, thorny thickets of the weed which are difficult to penetrate and largely devoid of native wildlife. An infestation near the Adelaide River outside the Park is reported to cover an area of about 4000 hectares. Fortunately, Kakadu is relatively free of this weed and so far only a few small outbreaks have been detected in the Park but the

Buffalo. (I.J.M.)

Sometimes buffalo get stuck in the mud. (I.J.M.)

97

possibility of a massive invasion remains. No effective means of biological control is known. Chemical control has been used but is expensive and undesirable in a national park.

The control strategy adopted in the Park is constant surveillance for early detection of any invasion, pulling out and destroying all weed plants found, fencing the infested area to keep out buffaloes which might spread any viable seed left in the ground and finally carrying out repeated inspections of the fenced area and destroying any germinating seedlings before they flower and set seed. The problem is unlikely to decrease whilst the weed is abundant outside the Park since seed will continue to be brought in by animals and on vehicles. Hopefully, the reduction in buffalo numbers will lessen the influx of seed from outside and diminish the area of disturbed land available for colonisation by *Mimosa*. The ultimate long-term solution may be biological control to eliminate, or at least control, the weed throughout tropical north Australia.

The aquatic fern *Salvinia molesta*, a native of Brazil, poses a serious threat to tropical freshwater communities throughout the world and there is great concern at its presence at Kakadu. Although sterile, it has an immense capacity in warm waters to reproduce rapidly by budding and to spread quickly. When prolific *Salvinia* clogs waterways and absorbs most of the nutrients from water to disadvantage the indigenous plants and animals. Attempts to control its spread by harvesting or by spraying with herbicides have not proved successful. The main hope is biological control using introduced insects to exterminate or at least keep any infestation in check. Weevils from Brazil have been used successfully elsewhere in Australia and in Papua New Guinea to control *Salvinia* and hopefully will do so at Kakadu. The use of control insects has been relatively effective in restricting another aquatic weed in tropical waters, water hyacinths *Eichhornia crassipes*. Fortunately, water hyacinths have not, as yet, been a serious problem at Kakadu.

Whilst biological control of weeds and pests through the introduction of exotic species is the best protective measure available to park management, it has to be used cautiously. There is always a danger that the introduced control agents will attack or harm native plants or animals to create a new pest problem. This happened in Queensland when cane toads *Bufo marinus* were introduced to combat insects damaging sugar cane plants. They proved not only ineffective in this regard, but were very destructive of native wildlife, partly because of their toxicity when eaten. The spread of cane toads from Queensland to the Northern Territory poses a serious threat to wildlife particularly in areas such as Kakadu. It is now accepted that before introducing alien species careful checks are needed to ensure the introductions will not have adverse effects and if necessary can be controlled.

■

Fire   Kakadu National Park has long been subjected to natural fires started by lightning and for thousands of years countless additional fires have been deliberately or accidentally lit by people. At the end of the dry season the smell of burning may be all pervading, and not until the intermittent rains of late November clear the air and quench any smouldering fires do new

Infestation of the weed *Salvinia* between lily leaves. (I.J.M.)

Flowers and seed pods of the weed *Mimosa*. (G.L.M.)

green shoots appear as the harbingers of the wet and the verdant greens to come.

Fires affect the structure, distribution pattern and composition of the vegetation and modify critical ecological processes such as organic turnover, nutrient circulation and vegetation succession. The fuel for the fires is plant matter accumulated during the wet season when plants grow rapidly and plant production exceeds decomposition. Deprived of water in the dry season, the plant biomass cures in the heat to become tinder dry and very inflammable. Then, when ignited, the organic matter burns readily and considerable heat is generated, particularly where much dead plant litter has accumulated over several years due to the temporary absence of fire. Fanned by the wind, uncontrolled

Wildfires are very destructive. (C.T.)

wildfires may spread widely and often rapidly, creating a blackened landscape and masking the countryside in a pall of smoke.

Some traditional Aboriginal reasons for lighting fires are well known, such as to hunt and drive kangaroos or to provide young tender shoots on which animals feed. Fires were also lit to clear vegetation away from camping places and to make it easier to walk through the bush. The purification roles of fire and smoke were important to Aboriginal people. There were traditional requirements to burn one's land, to keep it clean and to assert traditional land ownership authority. Aborigines also used fire to protect specific areas, for instance monsoon forests, which provide special food resources such as yams. The Aborigines burnt around the monsoon forest margins early in the dry season in the cooler months of May to July, knowing that in the prevailing climatic conditions fire would not penetrate into the forest. The perimeter burn then served as a fire break, stopping other fires entering the monsoon forests later in the year.

During pre-European times, sufficient Aboriginal people lived in, and moved around, Kakadu to carry out the traditional, systematic and more or less controlled firing program which produced a patchwork of small burns of different ages. Generally, Aborigines lit the fires during the early dry season up to early August. Normally such fires die out by the evening and since the scorch height up trees is then low, the tree flowers are protected to bear valuable fruit later. The fires were never so extensive nor so intense as to cause the widespread death of many native animals, which gained refuge in unburnt, or previously burnt, areas nearby. The net result at the end of each dry season was a complex mosaic of unburnt patches interspersed with small patches of low and medium intensity burns. These conditions reduced the likelihood of highly destructive wildfires burning out of control over large areas and generating great heat. Because the open forests, woodlands, grasslands and floodplains have been managed in this way for tens of thousands of years, the plant and animal communities now present are well adapted to a fire regime of patchy, but repeated, light burns.

The relatively recent, and more careless, attitude of Europeans towards fire results from failure to comprehend the long-term environmental consequences of late dry season burns. The fire regime of European times involves a shift from early to late dry season burning. This results in much larger and hotter burns, and greater damage to the biota. Recent studies at Kakadu indicate that repeated late dry season fires cause changes in the structure and composition of the vegetation. Tall annual grasses such as *Sorghum intrans* become more dominant and there is a substantial build-up of organic matter on the ground, resulting in hot burns which leave the ground bare and more subject to soil erosion. There is also a greater danger of wildfires burning out of control over large areas.

If the incidence of highly destructive, hot wildfires is to be reduced, the fire pattern of the immediate past needs to be replaced by one based on more traditional burns. Since the declaration of the Park, a policy has been introduced which involves having small patchy burns early in the dry season. These are carried out jointly with the traditional Aboriginal landowners. Experiments suggest these burns reduce grass growth, slow the build-up of litter on the ground and reduce the frequency of uncontrolled fires. Sometimes where controlled burning has to be done in remote locations it is necessary to drop incendiaries from aircraft or to use incendiary launchers carried on cross-country vehicles. In order to map fires and monitor fire management, records are made using landsat imagery from spacecraft.

Late season fires along the roadsides of Kakadu are often the start of serious and very damaging wildfires. Some of these fires are accidental, others are deliberately lit by people with little

Fire sequence in open eucalypt woodland. October 1980; immediately after a fire. (I.J.M.)

understanding of the consequences of their actions. To minimise this threat, roadside vegetation is burnt off by the Park staff.

For some Kakadu plant species fire is essential for successful seeding and regrowth and in general the vegetation seems adapted to a fire regime of light, patchy burns. The native cypress pine *Callitris columellaris* survives early dry season fires but quickly succumbs to high intensity, dry season fires during the hotter months of August to October. Most animals of the open woodland, such as kangaroos, wallabies, bandicoots and goannas, seem able to cope with limited burns and tend to concentrate on recently burnt areas where food is more readily available. Aboriginal stories attribute black kites, sometimes called smoke hawks, with the ability to pick up, fly with and drop burning sticks on unburnt areas to set fire to the vegetation and drive out into the open insects and other animals on which they prey.

Fire sequence in open eucalypt woodland. January 1981; plant growth has begun with the coming of the rains. (I.J.M.)

Understandably people coming to the Park are often concerned at seeing burnt areas and it is important to explain the reasons for deliberate burns. They need to appreciate that it appears impossible, and perhaps undesirable, to exclude fire from the Park and that wildfires are very destructive and within a few hours can negate the results of many years of nature protection. Based on the available knowledge, it seems for the time being that the best option is judicious and controlled use of fire as a management tool to prevent extensive wildfires without diminishing the variety of fire-tolerant plants and animals which together are part of the splendour of Kakadu.

Fire sequence in open eucalypt woodland. April 1981; the wet season has ended and a dense plant growth has developed. (I.J.M.)

Fire sequence in open eucalypt woodland. October 1981; at the end of the dry season the plant growth has died down. (I.J.M.)

The Park Headquarters is a meeting place and an administration and information centre. (R.G.)

At the reception desk visitors seek advice and information. (C.T.)

Tourism Tourism covers a wide range of recreational activities including travelling by coach or car, camping, fishing, walking, boating, photography and family picnics as well as viewing and learning about scenery, wildlife and cultural features. The past quarter of a century has seen an extraordinary expansion of tourism throughout the world. Actively promoted by governments, the tourist industry is seen as a growth industry providing economic and other benefits. National parks, in particular, have become meccas for people wishing to spend a relaxing vacation in an outdoor wilderness setting well away from urban pressures. In some regions, tourism based on national parks is the major industry and, being the primary contributor to the regional economy, provides opportunities for

Aboriginal children are keen to learn. (C.T.)

local people to gain new skills, improve their employment opportunities and participate in appropriate entrepreneurial activities.

Kakadu National Park is now recognised as an important tourist destination both regionally and nationally. The Aboriginal acquisition and management of Cooinda and the Border Store at Kakadu is evidence of their interest in participating in the tourist industry. At the same time, Aboriginal people arc cautious of a sudden and massive tourist development which might swamp their social and cultural traditions. They are also very conscious of the widespread desecration of Aboriginal burial places that occurred when European visitors first came to the area many years ago.

Wooden walkways protect the soil and are an outdoor classroom. (C.T.)

Before Kakadu National Park was proclaimed, there were comparatively few visitors and these were mainly Darwin residents interested in catching barramundi. Visitor surveys begun after proclamation have shown an average annual increase of about 16 per cent, with almost 60 000 people entering the Park in 1983. Most visitors come in the dry season, from May to October. With the inscription of Kakadu National Park on the World Heritage List and growing public interest in culture and nature, it seems inevitable that more people will want to enjoy and learn from Kakadu. People from Darwin are now being outnumbered by tourists from further afield in Australia and from overseas, particularly Europe and North America. These tourists are less interested in recreational fishing and wish to

Wooden shelters provide shade and information (C.T.)

learn about the natural and cultural history of the Park. Of necessity the Park management must anticipate and cater for an acceptable growth in tourism and for changing needs. Increasingly the demands on management will escalate, for example in rubbish disposal or the provision of more and better interpretation and accommodation facilities.

The tourist industry sees Kakadu as a tourism drawcard of immense potential benefit. Following proclamation, there has been a progressive increase in the Park of tourist accommodation of all kinds, from camping grounds and caravan parks to good hotels. Nevertheless, during peak tourist periods accommodation is at a premium. If tourist services and the use of the National Park are to develop in a rational way, close

A topographic model provides a bird's-eye view of the Park. (C.T.)

Historical photograph: a visiting
photographer in the 1920s.
(Australian Archives)

Picnic benches in tree shade are
popular. (C.T.)

A ranger helps visitors to understand
the Park. (C.T.)

co-operation is needed between the Park staff, Aborigines and
the various kinds of people involved with tourism, such as
hoteliers, coach drivers and tour operators. To foster this
co-operation, the Australian National Parks and Wildlife Service
has held seminars related to the tourist industry. These have
provided an opportunity to understand better the needs of
tourist operators and how they see tourism developing and to
inform the tourist trade of what the Park has to offer. Care is
needed to avoid tourist disappointment and disillusionment and
it is essential that promotional brochures given out by the
industry present an accurate picture of the Park.

Most people accept that national parks, like fine jewellery,
should not be kept locked up, unused and unseen. Some also
recognise that, as more people go to national parks, the
wilderness, cultural and other features attracting them may be
jeopardised and this could be exacerbated further by
promotional activities to make national parks more popular.
Both views have some validity in relation to Kakadu National
Park and it is essential to ensure that tourism and conservation
priorities are properly balanced. Kakadu National Park is so
large that it has a considerable and relatively untapped capacity
to enable people to better appreciate natural values.
Nevertheless, some land systems in the Park, such as the
floodplains, are very susceptible to disturbance and great care is
needed so as not to place in jeopardy native animals and plants.
More visitors to art sites pose similar conservation problems.
How best, and to what extent, the Park should be developed is a
matter of fine judgment.

Private contemplation of the work of nature. (C.T.)

Private contemplation of artwork. (C.T.)

Special interpretation displays, such as that at the Park Headquarters, provide an introduction to the Park and from comments received are appreciated by visitors. These displays have no damaging effects on park values. However, such displays can never substitute for personal viewing of park features and wildlife since outdoor involvement is an essential ingredient of the national park experience. Visitors who make the transition from the heat outside to the dark, cool shade of an Aboriginal shelter with its decorated walls and stand on the black sand of the ancient occupation soil can better imagine its previous inhabitants and how they lived. Very few national parks can provide such illuminating visions of the past. Park management has to plan for such experiences and other appropriate outdoor activities whilst minimising any adverse impacts of visitors.

Park management problems arise where people have divergent attitudes. Some place great emphasis on their personal comfort, others prefer to rough it and regard this as an essential part of an outdoor national park experience. The dilemma is highlighted by debate about whether or not first class hotels should be in the Park and, if so, where they should be located and what services they should provide. At a different level, a conflict of interest may arise at camping sites where someone sets up a power generator for electric light and refrigeration but the generator noise disturbs the tranquillity of other campers.

Other problems relate to access, which is increasingly difficult to control with the boom in four-wheel-drive, off-road vehicles and small boats powered by outboard motors. People have felt free to drive their vehicles anywhere in the Park without realising they may cause unintentional damage, for instance by disturbing wildlife or increasing soil erosion. Progressively the Park roads are being improved to encourage on-road driving. Improved roads and better access may be opposed by people accustomed to going to remote places of special interest and concerned that, with road upgrading, increased visitation will spoil their personal enjoyment of these places.

In practice, the Australian National Parks and Wildlife Service is obliged to control access in the long-term interests of the Park. For instance, access must be restricted where an area is being damaged by over-use, or to prevent interference with management research projects, or to protect wildlife and park features. Aboriginal people are willing to share the Park with others and agree to visitors seeing art galleries, but some places, such as sacred sites of great ceremonial or religious significance and dreaming and burial places, may have to be placed out of bounds. Furthermore, the privacy of people living in the Park, for instance Jabiru residents or Aborigines, may need to be safeguarded by limiting access to certain living areas.

One solution to the reconciliation of use conflicts lies in zoning the Park for different uses, for example wilderness, recreational and residential zones. A management regime based on park zonation must be sensitive to the attitudes of people, especially the traditional landowners, since much of Kakadu National Park is Aboriginal land.

Other management problems arise from visitor inexperience of wilderness conditions or their willingness to gamble that

Sunrise. (M.P.)

Evening scene. (M.P.)

disaster will not strike them. Some may undertake long distance bush walks in the Park with inadequate food, water and clothes. Others may drive to remote places in vehicles unreliable or unsuited to the conditions and do not inform anyone of their route. When people get into difficulty, the Park staff mounts massive, costly search and rescue operations which place heavy demands on the resources available for park management. Public safety is a prime concern of the Park staff but people often place themselves in danger unthinkingly. Despite posted warning signs, recreational fishermen and others enter rivers and billabongs, or camp on their banks, so placing themselves at risk of attack from crocodiles. The Australian National Parks and Wildlife Service recognises that controls are irksome and does

Evening water patrol. (C.T.)

not apply them without cause. Public understanding of control measures is being sought through a public information program emphasising the positive aspects of management and seeking the co-operation of all people in the interests of the Park.

■

Future Kakadu National Park presents unprecedented opportunities for people to appreciate the wonders of nature and of the development of human society and artistic creativity. All can benefit from the lessons they teach. The Australian National Parks and Wildlife Service feels privileged to have been given responsibility for the management of Kakadu National Park. The Service hopes that, under its custodianship and in co-operation with the traditional Aboriginal owners, Kakadu will remain an international treasure of great beauty and interest. Through wise and caring management, park values can and must be protected for this and future generations to enjoy.

FURTHER READING

Anon. 1980. *Kakadu National Park Plan of Management*. Australian National Parks and Wildlife Service, Canberra.

Anon. 1981. *The Heritage of Australia*. Macmillan, Melbourne.

Anon. 1984. *Aborigines and Uranium*. Australian Institute of Aboriginal Studies, Australian Government Publishing Service, Canberra.

Chaloupka, G. 1982. *Burrunguy Nourlangie Rock*. Northart.

Cogger, H. C. 1983. *Reptiles and Amphibians of Australia*. A. H. & A. W. Reed Pty Ltd, Frenchs Forest.

Edwards, R. 1979. *Australian Aboriginal Art, the Art of the Alligator Rivers Region, Northern Territory*. Australian Institute of Aboriginal Studies, Canberra.

Elliott, H. 1974. *Second World Conference on National Parks*. Arts Graphiques Heliographia SA, Lausanne.

Fox, R. W., Kelleher, G. G. and Kerr, C. B. 1976. *Ranger Uranium Environmental Inquiry, First Report*. Australian Government Publishing Service, Canberra.

Fox, R. W., Kelleher, G. G. and Kerr, C. B. 1977. *Ranger Uranium Environmental Inquiry, Second Report*. Australian Government Publishing Service, Canberra.

Frith, H. J. (Consultant editor). 1976. *Reader's Digest Complete Book of Australian Birds*. Reader's Digest Services Pty Ltd, Sydney.

Gillespie, D. 1983. *The Rock Art Sites of Kakadu National Park*. Special Publication No. 10, Australian National Parks and Wildlife Service, Canberra.

Gill, A. M., Groves, R. H. and Noble, I. R. (editors). 1981. *Fire and the Australian Biota*. Australian Academy of Science, Canberra.

Mulvaney, D. J. 1976. *The Prehistory of Australia*. Penguin Books, Sydney.

Ovington, J. D. 1978. *Australian Endangered Species, Mammals, Birds and Reptiles*. Cassell, Stanmore.

Peterson, N. and Langton, M. (editors). 1983. *Aborigines, Land and Land Rights*. Australian Institute of Aboriginal Studies, Canberra.

Schrire, C. 1982. *The Alligator Rivers, Prehistory and Ecology in Western Arnhem Land*, Terra Australis 7. Australian National University, Canberra.

Strahan, R. 1983. *Complete Book of Australian Mammals*. Angus and Robertson, Sydney.

Webb, L. J., Whitelock, D. and Brereton, J. Le Gay. 1969. *The Last of Lands*. Jacaranda Press, Milton.

Twin Falls. (C.T.)

INDEX OF SCIENTIFIC NAMES

Barn owl. (I.J.M.)

111

Jim Jim Gorge. (C.T.)

GENERAL INDEX